AMERICAN ORIENTAL SERIES

VOLUME 36

EARLY HEBREW ORTHOGRAPHY

A STUDY OF THE EPIGRAPHIC EVIDENCE

AMERICAN ORIENTAL SERIES

VOLUME 36

AMERICAN ORIENTAL SOCIETY
NEW HAVEN, CONNECTICUT
1952

EARLY HEBREW ORTHOGRAPHY

A STUDY OF THE EPIGRAPHIC EVIDENCE

BY

FRANK MOORE CROSS, JR.

AND

DAVID NOEL FREEDMAN

AMERICAN ORIENTAL SOCIETY

NEW HAVEN, CONNECTICUT

1952

MADE IN UNITED STATES OF AMERICA

J. H. FURST COMPANY, BALTIMORE, MARYLAND

PREFACE

The following monograph was prepared under the direction of Professor W. F. Albright, as the first of two joint doctoral dissertations presented to The Johns Hopkins University by the writers. It is hoped that the second part of the work will be ready in the near future.

We are indebted to Professor Albright for the inspiration which suggested the present study, and for his constant and patient assistance which made possible its completion. We also should like to thank Professor F. R. Blake, our kindly and learned mentor in linguistic problems.

FRANK MOORE CROSS, JR.
DAVID NOEL FREEDMAN.

TABLE OF CONTENTS

INTRODUCTION

THE INCONSISTENCIES in the orthography of the Hebrew Bible had been noted and puzzled over long before the advent of modern scientific scholarship. From early times, scribes and grammarians concerned themselves with the correct spelling of words, the proper indication of the *'immōt haqrī'ā* (*matres lectionis*). These labors continued over a period of a thousand years, and culminated in the monumental work of the Massoretes. Although persistent efforts were made to standardize the orthography of the Bible, they were never completely successful, and clear evidence of the earlier stages of the development of Hebrew spelling has been preserved in the text. Thus the Hebrew Bible which tradition has delivered to us is in reality a palimpsest; underlying the visible text, the varied spelling customs of older ages have been recorded.

Modern scholarly efforts to analyze the evolution of Hebrew orthography began with Wilhelm Gesenius and the decipherment of the Phoenician inscriptions in the early 19th century.[1] Gesenius was the first scholar to make serious application of the evidence derived from inscriptional data to biblical orthography. The general principles he laid down in 1815,[2] remained standard until the work of Nöldeke more than fifty years later. Valuable contributions were made in the intervening years by Ewald, Olshausen, Lagarde and Wellhausen,[3] among others, but they only modified Gesenius' position in detail.

[1] *Scripturae Linguaeque Phoeniciae*, Leipzig, 1837. Gesenius had been working on the Phoenician inscriptions for many years, and had long since satisfied himself as to the basic principles of Phoenician orthography, cf. pp. 56-59.

[2] W. Gesenius, *Geschichte der hebräischen Sprache und Schrift*, Leipzig, 1815, pp. 182 ff. His view was that originally Hebrew writing was largely defective, like Phoenician, but that from relatively early times, vowel letters were in use. He distinguished three *matres lectionis*: *yodh*, *waw*, and *aleph*.

[3] H. Ewald, *Ausführliches Lehrbuch der hebräischen Sprache*, 8th ed., Göttingen, 1870, pp. 48-52. The material he presents appeared as early as 1826 in the first edition of the work. J. Olshausen, *Lehrbuch der hebräischen Sprache*, Braunschweig, 1861, §§ 31, 38, 39. P. Lagarde, *Anmerkungen zur griechischen Übersetzung der Proverbien*, Leipzig, 1863, p. 4. He observed that in many cases where the Septuagint differed from the Massoretic text, the difference could be explained most easily on the supposition that vowel letters were not used in the Hebrew *Vorlage* of the Greek translation. He came to the drastic and untenable conclusion that no *matres lectionis* appeared in the Hebrew text at the time the Septuagint was made. J. Wellhausen, *Der Text der Bücher Samuelis*, Göttingen, 1871, pp. 17 ff., refuted Lagarde's contention. He pointed out that the evidence of the LXX showed only that the distribution of *matres lectionis* in the *Vorlage* may have been different from that in the Massoretic text. He asserted that in

The first major studies of Hebrew orthography followed the discovery of the Meša' Stone in 1868. On the basis of the new evidence, Nöldeke[4] demonstrated that final vowel letters were already in common use in the 9th century B. C., but that internal *matres lectionis* had not yet appeared. He further noted that the diphthongs *aw* and *ay* were represented regularly by *waw* and *yodh*, and argued from this that the preservation of these signs in the orthography after the contraction of the diphthongs was the source of internal *matres lectionis.* He also established that in addition to *waw* and *yodh*, *he* commonly was used as a final vowel letter in early times, but not *aleph* which remained a true consonant in the final position until much later.

In 1876, Daniel Chwolson presented a brilliant though erratic study of the *matres lectionis* in old Hebrew orthography.[5] His chief contention was:

> Man kann *a priori* behaupten, dass die Hebräer *ursprünglich* diese Buchstaben in der Mitte oder am Ende des Wortes eben so wenig gebraucht haben wie die Phönizier, von denen man positiv weiss, dass die Vocalbuchstaben bei ihnen erst in verhältnissmässig später Zeit und allmählig eingeführt wurden; denn man hat, unseres Erachtens, absolut gar keinen Grund anzunehmen, dass die alten Hebräer, welche dasselbe Alfabet wie die Phönizier gebraucht und eine von der Sprache derselben fast nur dialectisch verschiedene Mundart gesprochen haben, eine nur ihnen allein eigenthümliche Orthographie gebraucht haben sollten. Es kann ja auch nicht angenommen werden, dass die *alten* Hebräer, zur Zeit als die hebräischen Sprache noch eine lebendige war, ein grösseres Bedürfniss gehabt haben sollten, ihre Schrift deutlicher zu machen, als die Phönizier.[6]

Chwolson held that vowel letters were not used generally until after the decline of Hebrew as a living language, although he correctly surmised that the introduction of final *matres lectionis* preceded that of medial *matres lectionis.*[7] Consequently, he thought that the greater part of the

all probability more vowel letters appeared in the texts of the Maccabaean age than later. For an admirable discussion of the history of this subject in the nineteenth century, see Leo Bardowicz, *Studien zur Geschichte der Orthographie des Althebräischen*, Frankfurt a. M., 1894, pp. 21-36.

[4] T. Nöldeke, *Die Inschrift des Königs Mesa von Moab*, Kiel, 1870, pp. 31 ff. See also his review of Wellhausen's book (Note 3) in the *Zeitschrift für wissenschaftliche Theologie*, XVI (1873), pp. 120 ff.

[5] Die Quiescentes הוי in der althebraeischen Orthographie," *Travaux de la troisième session du Congrès International des Orientalistes, St. Pétersbourg 1876*, II, St. Petersburg and Leiden, 1879, pp. 457-490.

[6] *Ibid.*, p. 459.

[7] Although he apparently recognized that there were final *matres lectionis* in the Meša' inscription, he discounted most of them as true consonants. It did not affect his view therefore that even final vowel letters were used only sporadically in the biblical texts until a very late date. Cf. pp. 475 ff.

Old Testament originally was written in accordance with the consonantal principles of Phoenician orthography. Later scribes inserted vowel letters in the text, to clarify the meaning and fix the pronunciation of the words. They did not always succeed in their task, however, and frequently failed to reproduce correctly the grammatical forms of the older spoken language.[8] In dealing with difficult passages, Chwolson proposed to disregard all *matres lectionis* as secondary, and reconstruct the original Hebrew of the author on the basis of the consonantal text alone. He applied his methods indiscriminately, treating the earliest poetry of the Bible and late books like Chronicles as though they belonged to the same orthographic stratum, and assembled a heterogeneous collection of only superficially related materials. The results which he obtained were largely worthless, as a consequence.[9] Nevertheless, Chwolson was the first to grasp the implications of the study of historical orthography for the analysis of the biblical text, and to demonstrate the potential value of this exegetical tool.

About the same time, a more sober and systematic treatment of the subject was given by Bernhard Stade.[10] He laid down the following principles. Alphabetic writing in Semitic originated as a purely consonantal system. *Matres lectionis* developed regularly from historical spelling, in which the consonantal sign was preserved although it no longer represented the original consonantal sound. These vowel letters first appeared in the final position, and indicated long vowels which resulted from the contraction of diphthongs, the syncope of intervocalic *he, waw* and *yodh,* and the general breakdown of inflectional endings. Medial vowel letters were a later development, but also arise from historical spelling. Once the function of the vowel letter was fixed, its use was extended to other words and forms where there was no historical basis for its employment. At the same time, the *mater lectionis* might represent two or more different vowel sounds.[11]

[8] Chwolson reconstructed older Hebrew largely on the basis of classical Arabic (pp. 481 ff.). He rejected the idea that certain peculiar forms preserved in the Massoretic text were due to Aramaic influence, but regarded them rather as survivals of archaic Hebrew morphology (pp. 487 ff.).

[9] His material consists mainly in examples of scribal lapses, or real variant readings, and has nothing to do with defective orthography.

[10] *Lehrbuch der hebräischen Grammatik*, Leipzig, 1879, pp. 34-38.

[11] Stade does not distinguish historically among the values which a *mater lectionis* might have, nor does he recognize any difference in orthographic usage depending upon whether the vowel letter occurs in the final or medial position. Thus he assigns the values *ô* and *û* to *waw*. While this is a correct description of the actual situation in the Massoretic text, it does not do justice to the long history of development in the sign's usage. Originally, the use of *waw* as a *mater lectionis* was restricted to the final position, and the value, *ū*. Later it was used

Stade explained the origin of *he* as a *mater lectionis* on the basis of the so-called *he locale*, which he regarded as originally consonantal.[12] *Waw* and *yodh* developed as vowel letters through the historical spelling of contracted diphthongs, or the coalescence of semi-vowels and homogeneous vowel sounds.[13] He also correctly maintained that *aleph* was not used as a *mater lectionis* until a much later period.

Stade based his analysis of Hebrew orthography largely on the evidence of the Meša' inscription, rather than the late Phoenician materials. The subsequent discovery of the Siloam inscription offered confirmation of Stade's view that Hebrew orthography of that period more closely resembled Moabite than Phoenician orthography.

Scholarly opinion has for the most part accepted Stade's principles, and scholarly work since his time has been confined to refinements and minor modifications of his position. Subsequent students of the subject added little to the general picture. No adequate historical treatment of the evolution of the *'immōt haqrī'ā* appeared, to replace Stade's vague relative chronology.[14] Grimme[15] and Bardowicz[16] presented little of current interest in dealing with the development of Hebrew orthography.

in the medial position, and represented both *ū* and *ô* < *aw*. This secondary value, *ô*, was then transferred to *waw* in the final position, and it ultimately displaced *he* in that position as the sign for *ô* (though there are numerous survivals of *he* = *ô* in the present text).

[12] *Ibid.*, p. 35. H. Grimme, *Grundzüge der hebraeischen Akzent- und Vokallehre*, Freiburg, 1896, pp. 6-7, criticizes this view on the grounds that the so-called *he locale* is not consonantal and marks only the accusative ending. Evidence from Ugaritic shows that the *he* in this case was originally consonantal, but the time of its quiescence in Hebrew cannot be determined, and the problem remains unsettled. Grimme also rejects the view that the *he* as a *mater lectionis* is derived from the feminine ending (*at* > **ah* > *ā*), denying that the middle form with consonantal *he* ever existed. He holds that the use of *he* as a vowel letter originates in the historical spelling of the pronominal suffix of the third person.

[13] Stade, *op. cit.*, p. 35: *iy* > *î*, *ay* > *ê*, represented by *yodh*; *uw* > *û*, *aw* > *ô*, represented by *waw*. Cf. note 11.

[14] Cf. C. D. Ginsburg, *Introduction to the Massoretico-Critical Edition of the Hebrew Bible*, London, 1897, pp. 137-157. His position approximates that of Chwolson with respect to the absence of *matres lectionis* in the earlier texts of the Old Testament. He supports his case with examples of vowel-letter omission in the final and medial positions, derived from the Massorah. The value of his work seriously is weakened by his failure to distinguish historical periods in the development of Hebrew orthography.

[15] *Op. cit.*, pp. 5-8.

[16] L. Bardowicz, *Studien zur Geschichte des Orthographie des Althebräischen*, Frankfort a. M., 1894. See also his shorter treatment, "Das allmähliche Ueberhandnehmen der *matres lectionis* im Bibeltexte," *Monatsschrift für Geschichte und Wissenschaft des Judenthums* 38 (1894), pp. 117-121, 157-167. Bardowicz deals principally with the rabbinic and talmudic periods, comparing biblical quo-

Kautzsch, in successive editions of the Gesenius Grammar,[17] simply adopted Stade's main arguments. S. R. Driver discussed the subject in the light of the extant inscriptions, but his work marked no particular advance over that of his predecessors.[18]

In 1916, Alfred Rahlfs published a major essay on the *matres lectionis* in the Old Testament.[19] In this paper he treated at length the distinction between the phonetic principle of Phoenician orthography, and the conservative tendency toward historical spelling in Moabite, and more particularly in Hebrew. He ascribed the origin of all *matres lectionis* to historical spelling. The general inconsistency of their use in all Canaanite dialects he attributed to the continual conflict between phonetic and historical orthography. On one side there was persistent pressure for spelling which corresponded to pronunciation, and on the other a conservative inertia which tended to preserve the older orthography. According to Rahlfs, the use of *matres lectionis* was sporadic at first, then gradually but steadily increased. They were used in order to distinguish words and forms which fell together in the consonantal orthography. Rahlfs' frequently repeated justification for this procedure is "die Rücksicht auf das Verständniss." The more consistent use of final *matres lectionis*, as against medial *matres lectionis*, is due to the fact that the most decisive inflectional differences involve final vowels.[20]

Rahlfs' involved analysis of the origin of *he* as a vowel letter has much to commend it, as against the arbitrary discussions of Stade and Brockelmann.[21] Brockelmann, followed more recently by Bergsträsser[22]

tations in the Talmud with the Massoretic text, as to the use and frequency of *matres lectionis.*

[17] Kautzsch was responsible for the 22nd through the 28th editions (1878-1909) of *Wilhelm Gesenius' hebräische Grammatik*, Leipzig.

[18] *Notes on the Hebrew Text and the Topography of the Books of Samuel*, 2nd ed., Oxford, 1913, pp. xxvii-xxxiii.

[19] "Zur Setzung der Lesemütter im Alten Testament," *Nachrichten von der Königlichen Gesellschaft der Wissenschaften zu Göttingen*, Philologisch-historische Klasse, 1916, pp. 315-347.

[20] Rahlfs lumps together the evidence for final *matres lectionis* found in late Phoenician inscriptions, the Meša' Stone and the Siloam Inscription. A much greater consistency in the use of final *matres lectionis* obtains than he is willing to admit. Few, if any, occur in Phoenician until very late times; the cases he finds are the result of erroneous interpretation. The instances of the omission of the final vowel letter in the Moabite and Hebrew inscriptions, which he adduces, are also due to misinterpretation of the material. He does not take into account the effect of the long history of the final *matres lectionis* in standardizing their usage, as against the comparatively late development of internal vowel letters.

[21] *Grundriss der vergleichenden Grammatik der semitischen Sprachen*, I: *Laut- und Formenlehre*, Berlin, 1908, § 225, esp. p. 409, n. 1.

[22] *Hebräische Grammatik*, I, Leipzig, 1918, p. 45.

and Kahle,[23] maintains that the pausal form of the feminine noun is the logical source of *he* as a *mater lectionis* (i. e., *-*ah* > *ā*, written historically with final *he*). Rahlfs is nearer the truth in his comment, ". . . wo man einen vokalischen Ausgang mit Nachdruck spricht, kann hinter ihm leicht ein Hauchlaut entstehen," [24] though perhaps this homogeneity of *he* with most vowel sounds simply explains its flexibility and wide usefulness as a vowel letter. His rejection of the feminine ending with supposed consonantal *he* as the origin of the *he* used as a *mater lectionis* is based, however, not upon an analysis of the questionable phonetic equation involved (-*at* > *-*ah* > *ā*), but on other, fallacious grounds. He holds that because in the Mešaʿ inscription, feminine nouns regularly end in -*t*, while at the same time *he* is used as a *mater lectionis* at the end of other words, the scholar must therefore seek the origin of this usage in other forms. In his rigid view that historical spelling provides the only explanation for the origin and use of vowel letters, Rahlfs completely overlooks the possibility that in Moabite, orthographic practices in the representation of final vowels may have been borrowed from another language. Rahlfs' "isolationism," in which he is joined by nearly all other scholars,[25] is reflected by the fact that he fails to bring into the discussion of the history of orthography the Aramaic inscriptional material.

Rahlfs ascribes the insertion or omission of *matres lectionis* to optional decision on the part of scribes as to whether or not a word or form was ambiguous. This attitude disregards the powerful force of convention which stabilized spelling fashions in consistent phonetic schemes for long periods (in the case of Phoenician, for almost the whole of its long history). Moreover, Rahlfs' failure to deal adequately with the historical development of the Canaanite language gives his study a curiously flat perspective. He gathers his materials from disparate sources, without discriminating between early and late, normal and archaizing orthography. As a result, his evidence is organized into historically meaningless categories.[26]

[23] Kahle wrote the pertinent sections in Bauer and Leander's *Historische Grammatik der hebräischen Sprache des Alten Testaments*, Halle a. S., 1922. Cf. p. 91.

[24] *Op. cit.*, p. 330.

[25] A notable exception is F. R. Blake. See his discussion of the matter in "The Development of Symbols for the Vowels in the Alphabets derived from the Phoenician," *JAOS* 60 (1940), pp. 391-413; note especially p. 397, where he suggests that the system of *matres lectionis* may have been developed in a single language and then extended to others.

[26] It should be noted, however, that the historical grammar of the Canaanite dialects was not very far advanced at the time he wrote (1916).

Subsequent treatments of the subject in the standard grammars[27] follow conventional lines, and require no special notice.[28] The radically different views of some present-day scholars will be discussed in the body of the paper.

The enormously enlarged fund of epigraphic material in Northwest Semitic discovered in the past few decades has made necessary a complete transformation of older ideas regarding the history of early orthographic developments. No longer must the scholar depend upon a few hints from partly misunderstood inscriptions, and develop his views with the aid of subjectively derived principles of evolution. These new materials have provided a solid basis for the inductive study of orthography, leading to the determination of the fundamental laws governing its history and practice.

General questions of chronology in the Near East after 1500 B. C. have largely been cleared up. The accurate dating of finds on the basis of stratigraphy and typology, and the fixing of the various stages in the evolution of the Canaanite alphabet, have made possible the historical analysis of orthographic development. The reconstruction of the linguistic history of Canaanite has been facilitated greatly by the discovery of the Ugaritic mythological corpus, as well as much new inscriptional material. The use of transcriptional evidence in other languages, and the rigorous application of the methods of comparative philology have also contributed. It cannot be too strongly emphasized that an historical study of orthography is impossible until inscriptions have been dated accurately and interpreted satisfactorily. At the same time, as orthographic principles and usages are defined, they become an invaluable tool in determining the refinements of linguistic change and development. The two disciplines increasingly complement each other.

The large number of inscriptions and other epigraphic remains now available provide an adequate basis for valid generalizations, inductively arrived at. They also make possible the study of the interrelationships of the orthographic systems of different dialect groups at various stages in their development.

There can no longer be any doubt that the proto-Canaanite alphabet originated as a purely consonantal form of writing. While the decipherment of the oldest inscriptions in this alphabet has not yet reached cer-

[27] See the treatments by Bergsträsser, *op. cit.*, pp. 44-46, and 94 ff., and Kahle in Bauer and Leander's Hebrew grammar, pp. 91 ff.

[28] The most recent general study is the short article by W. Chomsky, "The History of our Vowel-System in Hebrew," *JQR*, N. S. 32 (1941-42), pp. 27-49. He follows Stade.

tainty in all cases (due in large part to the fragmentary nature of the finds), some conclusions as to their orthography can be drawn.[29]

The earliest known alphabetic writing is represented by the Gezer Potsherd (ca. 1700 B.C.),[30] the proto-Sinaitic inscriptions (ca. 1500 B.C.),[31] discovered by Petrie and succeeding Finnish and American expeditions, the Lachish Dagger (ca. 1500 B.C.),[32] the Beth-Shemesh Ostracon (13th century B.C.),[33] the Lachish Ewer (I) and Lachish Bowl # 1 (II) (late 13th century B.C.),[34] the Archaic Byblian Inscription (ca. 1200 B.C.),[35] the Tell el-Ḥesi Potsherd (12th century B.C.?),[36]

[29] There is a very extensive literature on the proto-Canaanite alphabetic inscriptions. Some recent general treatments are listed here: S. Yeivin, "The Palestino-Sinaitic Inscriptions," *PEFQS*, 1937, pp. 180-193. He deals with the early Palestinian material. J. W. Flight, "The Present State of Studies in the History of Writing in the Near East," Chapter IV in *The Haverford Symposium on Archaeology and the Bible*, Elihu Grant ed., New Haven, 1938, pp. 111-135. T. Böhl, "Die Sichem-Plakette," *ZDPV* 61 (1938), pp. 1-25, includes a general survey of Palestinian finds. B. Maisler, "Zur Urgeschichte des phoenizisch-hebraeischen Alphabets," *JPOS* XVIII (1938), pp. 278-291. D. Diringer, "The Palestinian Inscriptions and the Origin of the Alphabet," *JAOS* 63 (1943), pp. 24-30. A. Bea, "Die Entstehung des Alphabets," *Miscellanea Giovanni Mercati*, VI (1946), pp. 1-35.

[30] References to the different epigraphic materials will be found in the literature indicated above. Additional information on the Gezer Potsherd may be found in the following articles: W. R. Taylor, "The New Gezer Inscription," *JPOS* 10 (1930), pp. 79-81, and "Some New Palestinian Inscriptions," *BASOR* # 41 (1931), pp. 27-28; W. F. Albright, "The Inscription from Gezer at the School in Jerusalem," *BASOR* # 58 (1935), pp. 28-29.

[31] A survey of the material and a convenient bibliography will be found in the definitive article by W. F. Albright, "The Early Alphabetic Inscriptions from Sinai and their Decipherment," *BASOR* # 110 (1948), pp. 6-22.

[32] Cf. J. L. Starkey, "Excavations at Tell ed-Duweir," *PEFQS*, 1937, pp. 228-241; J. Obermann, "The Archaic Inscriptions from Lachish," *JAOS* 58 (1938), Supplement, pp. 1-48.

[33] E. Grant, "Découvert épigraphique à Beth Šemeš," *RB* 39 (1930), pp. 401-402. W. F. Albright, "The Inscription from Gezer at the School in Jerusalem," pp. 28-29, and *The Archaeology of Palestine and the Bible*, New York, 1935, pp. 50, 86, and n. 74.

[34] T. H. Gaster, "The Archaic Inscriptions" chapter in *Lachish II, The Fosse Temple*, ed. by Tufnell, Inge and Harding, Oxford University Press, 1940, pp. 49-57; and "The Tell Duweir Ewer Inscription," *PEFQS* 1934, pp. 176-178. E. Burrows, "The Tell Duweir Ewer Inscription," *PEFQS*, 1934, pp. 179-180. W. F. Albright, "The Early Evolution of the Hebrew Alphabet," *BASOR* # 63 (1936), pp. 8-12. J. Obermann, "The Archaic Inscriptions from Lachish," *loc. cit.*

[35] M. Dunand, "Une nouvelle inscription énigmatique," *Mélanges Maspero* I, Fasc. 2 (1935-38), pp. 567-571. W. F. Albright, "The So-called Enigmatic Inscription from Byblus," *BASOR* # 116 (1949), pp. 12-14.

[36] W. F. Albright, "A Neglected Hebrew Inscription of the Thirteenth Century B.C.," *AfO* V (1929), pp. 150-152. This inscription is now to be dated in the 12th century.

the Megiddo Bracelet (12th century B. C.?)[37] and the Ruweiseh Arrowhead (end of the 11th century B. C.)[38]

While in the past there has been some doubt, it is now certain that the alphabet was derived acrophonically, under direct or indirect Egyptian influence, with a center of radiation somewhere in Canaan, probably in Phoenicia proper. This alphabet was the ancestor of the standard Phoenician, Aramaic and early Hebrew scripts, on one hand, and the different South Semitic scripts on the other.[39] The inventor of the North Canaanite cuneiform alphabet (represented primarily in the Ugaritic tablets, but also in fragments from Palestine) obviously was acquainted with the principles of "phonetic consonantism," and, as has now been demonstrated, was familiar with the proto-Canaanite alphabet.[40] The Ugaritic script, however, was not a conscious imitation of the proto-Canaanite, as is clearly indicated by new data on the evolution of the proto-Canaanite alphabet.[41] Resemblances between the 15th century

[37] P. L. O. Guy and R. M. Engberg, *Megiddo Tombs*, Chicago, 1938, pp. 173-176.

[38] P.-E. Guigues, "Pointe de flèche en bronze a inscription phénicienne," *Mélanges de l'Université Saint-Joseph* XI (1926), pp. 323-328. S. Ronzevalle, "Note sur le texte phénicien de la flèche publiée par M. P.-E. Guigues," *ibid.*, pp. 329-358; and R. Dussaud, review of the previous articles in *Syria* VIII (1927), pp. 185-186. More recently two sherds have been discovered bearing inscriptions in the proto-Canaanite alphabet. Unfortunately these are too fragmentary to be read; cf. Ruth B. Kallner, "שתי כתובות על גבי חרסים," "Two Inscribed Sherds from Tell eṣ-Ṣarem" (English Title), *Kedem* II (1945), pp. 11 ff. E. L. Sukenik, "הערה לחרס מתל אץ צארם," "Note on the Sherd from Tell eṣ-Ṣarem" (English Title), *Kedem* II (1945), p. 15, dates the inscriptions in the 13th–12th centuries B. C. In addition there is a small group of inscriptions of uncertain nature, or written in a different kind of alphabet. To this group belong the Tell el-'Ajjul Sherd, cf. F. Petrie, *Ancient Gaza* II, London, 1931-34, pl. 30; the Shechem Plaque, cf. Böhl, "Die Sichem-Plakette"; the Lachish Bowl # 2, cf. Gaster, "The Archaic Inscriptions," pp. 49-57; the Lachish Censer Lid, cf. Starkey, *PEFQS* 1936, pp. 178-189; and the Balu'ah Stele, cf. G. Horsfield and L. H. Vincent, "Une stèle Egypto-Moabite au *Balou'a*," *RB* 41 (1932), pp. 417-444; for a different view of this stele see Albright, "The Early Evolution of the Hebrew Alphabet," *BASOR* # 63, p. 11.

[39] So Albright, "The Early Evolution of the Hebrew Alphabet," *BASOR* # 63, p. 11. A contrary view is taken by M. Dunand, *Byblia Grammata*, Beyrouth, 1945, pp. 171 ff.

[40] Cf. W. F. Albright, "Some Important Recent Discoveries: Alphabetic Origins and the Idrimi Statue," *BASOR* # 118 (1950), pp. 11-20.

[41] In his article, "The Early Alphabetic Inscriptions from Sinai and their Decipherment," Albright confirms the 18th Dynasty date of these inscriptions first proposed by Petrie, against the commonly accepted 12th Dynasty date. This brings the proto-Sinaitic alphabet down to within a century of the Ugaritic alphabet, and removes from consideration hitherto supposed resemblances between the Ugaritic forms and later forms of the Canaanite alphabet. The proto-Sinaitic and Ugaritic alphabets have practically nothing noticeable in common.

Ras Shamrah alphabet and the later Phoenician alphabet are purely coincidental.[42]

As indicated above, the orthography of all extant proto-Canaanite inscriptions is purely consonantal in character.[43] This fact is attested by the persistence of consonantal orthography in a number of languages which derived their scripts from proto-Canaanite. Thus the earliest inscriptions in standard Phoenician, the earliest Hebrew exemplar, as well as the epigraphic remains of Minaeo-Sabaean, Thamudic, Lihyanic, Safaitic and Old Ethiopic are consistently consonantal in orthography.[44] It follows that this was originally the case with all Semitic dialects which adopted the proto-Canaanite alphabet; modifications in the consonantal principle would occur in the course of time. In the case of Aramaic in particular, adjustments in orthography (i. e., the introduction of *matres lectionis*) seem to have been made almost immediately.[45]

In the following treatment of the history of early Hebrew orthography, we shall deal first with the Phoenician inscriptions from Byblus, and the Kilamuwa inscription from Zinčirli. These inscriptions set forth the unqualified consonantal scheme which influenced scribal practice in Israel, or more precisely, they are the clearest examples of the system of orthography adopted in early Hebrew. The next section will treat early Aramaic orthography. This material has never adequately been treated, despite its prime importance for the understanding of the origin and development of *matres lectionis*. In this discussion, we shall analyze the Aramaic inscriptions dating from about 900-700 B. C. The later developments are of little significance for the study of the Hebrew orthography of the period of our main interest. Before turning to the early Hebrew materials, we shall consider the evidence of the Moabite Stone, and the relationship between its orthography and that of Hebrew. Hebrew epigraphic material will be studied in detail, beginning with the Gezer Calendar (ca. 925 B. C.), and continuing through the Lachish Letters (589 B. C.), or down to the time of the Exile. A concluding section will sketch briefly the subsequent history of Hebrew spelling, with an account of the later orthographic revisions which affected the text of the Bible, until it was permanently fixed in the period of the Massoretes.

42 Cf. Dunand, *Byblia Grammata*, pp. 180 ff. He points out that the Ugaritic signs are made by the simplest possible combination of vertical, horizontal, diagonal and corner wedges, and that this must have been the guiding principle of the inventor. This is also Albright's view.

43 The successful partial interpretation of the proto-Sinaitic inscriptions by Albright assures that this principle is correct. Supporting evidence is offered by the Ugaritic tablets, the orthography of which is purely consonantal.

44 See F. R. Blake, "The Development of Symbols for the Vowels in the Alphabets Derived from the Phoenician," p. 396, n. 9.

45 For a discussion of Aramaic orthography, see Chapter II.

Chapter I

EARLY PHOENICIAN ORTHOGRAPHY

The materials treated in this section include the Bronze Spatula Inscription (ca. 1000 B. C.), the Sarcophagus Inscription of Aḥiram (early 10th century), the inscriptions of Yeḥimilk (middle of the 10th century), Abibaal (ca. 925 B. C.), Elibaal (ca. 915 B. C.), and Shipiṭbaal (end of the 10th century), and the 'Abda' Sherd (ca. 900 B. C.), all from Byblus;[1] and in addition, the Kilamuwa Inscription from Zinčirli (ca. 825 B. C.).[2] Although the Aḥiram Inscription was discovered more

[1] For the early Phoenician inscriptions, note the following original publications, or official editions.

For the Bronze Spatula Inscription:
M. Dunand, *Fouilles de Byblos,* I (Atlas), Paris, 1937, Plate XXXII, p. 1125 a and b, photograph; II (Texte), Paris, 1939, p. 28, handcopy; "Spatule de bronze avec épigraphe phénicienne du XIIIe siècle," *Bulletin du Musée de Beyrouth,* II (1938), pp. 99-107.

For the Aḥiram Inscription:
R. Dussaud, "Les inscriptions phéniciennes du tombeau d'Ahiram, roi de Byblos," *Syria* V (1924), pp. 135-157, with three plates. P. Montet, *Byblos et l'Égypte* (Texte), Paris, 1928, pp. 236-238; (Atlas), Paris, 1929, Plates CXXXVIII-CXL.

For the Yeḥimilk Inscription:
M. Dunand, "Nouvelle inscription phénicienne archaïque," *RB* 39 (1930), pp. 321-331, with plate; *Fouilles de Byblos,* I, Plate XXXI; II, p. 30.

For the Abibaal Inscription:
Ch. Clermont-Ganneau, *Recueil d'Archéologie Orientale,* VI (Paris, 1905), pp. 74-78, and photograph. R. Dussaud, "Les inscriptions phéniciennes du tombeau d'Ahiram, roi de Byblos," pp. 145-147.

For the Elibaal Inscription:
R. Dussaud, "Dédicace d'une statue d'Osorkon Ier par Eliba'al, roi de Byblos," *Syria* VI (1925), pp. 101-117. P. Montet, *Byblos et l'Égypte* I (Texte), pp. 49-54; II (Atlas), Plates XXXVI-XXXVII. M. Dunand, *Fouilles de Byblos* II (Texte), pp. 17 ff., for additional material.

For the Shipiṭbaal Inscription:
M. Dunand, *Byblia Grammata,* Beyrouth, 1945, pp. 146-151, with plates.

For the 'Abda' Inscription:
M. Dunand, *Byblia Grammata,* pp. 152-155, with plate.

For general bibliography following the original publications, see Montet, *Byblos et l'Égypte,* and Z. Harris, *A Grammar of the Phoenician Language,* New Haven, 1936. For more recent bibliography, see Dunand, *Byblia Grammata,* and W. F. Albright, "The Phoenician Inscriptions of the Tenth Century B. C. from Byblus," *JAOS* 67 (1947), pp. 153-160. There has also appeared a short article by C. Brockelmann, "Kanaanäische Miscellen," in the *Festschrift Otto Eissfeldt,* Halle, 1947, pp. 61-67.

[2] There is a considerable literature on the Kilamuwa Inscription. Among the more important treatments are the following: F. von Luschan, *Ausgrabungen in Sendschirli* IV, Berlin, 1911, pp. 374-377 (the original publication). E. Littmann, "Die Inschriften des Königs Kalumu," *Sitzungsberichte der Preussischen Akademie der Wissenschaften,* 1911, ppp. 976-985. F. E. Peiser, "Die neue Inschrift

than twenty-five years ago, and the Kilamuwa Inscription has been known since 1911, this body of early Phoenician writing was not adequately understood until recent years.

The principles of early Phoenician orthography have been analyzed effectively by Zellig Harris,[3] and W. F. Albright in his definitive treatment of the Byblian inscriptions. We shall not attempt to do more than illustrate the well-established orthographic system of early Phoenician, pointing out those words which have special significance for the study of orthography as they occur in the inscriptions. Attempts to vocalize must be made on the basis of other Canaanite dialects, particularly Hebrew and Punic, and from transliterations in other systems of writing.[4] The Kilamuwa Inscription, which dates after the major phase of Phoenician influence on Hebrew orthography, has been selected from among other contemporary Phoenician inscriptions,[5] because of its particular bearing on the discussion of Aramaic orthography.[6]

aus Sendschirli," *OLZ* XIV (1911), col. 540-545. C. Brockelmann, "Zu den Inschriften des Königs Kalumu," *Sitzungsberichte der Preussischen Akademie der Wissenschaften*, 1911, p. 1142-1146. M. J. Lagrange, "La nouvelle inscription de Sendjirly," *RB* NS 9 (1912), pp. 253-259. J. Halévy, "Les inscriptions du roi Kalumu," *Revue Sémitique* XX (1912), pp. 19-30. J. Hehn, "Die Inschrift des Königs Kalumu," *Biblische Zeitschrift*, 1912, pp. 113-124. M. Lidzbarski, *Ephemeris für semitische Epigraphik* III (1909-1915), Giessen, 1915, pp. 218-238. H. Bauer, "Die כלמו Inschrift aus Sendschirli," *ZMDG* 67 (1913), pp. 684-691; *ZDMG* 68 (1914), pp. 227 ff. C. C. Torrey, "The Zakar and Kalamu Inscriptions," *JAOS* 35 (1915-17), pp. 353-369. W. F. Albright, "Notes on Early Hebrew and Aramaic Epigraphy," *JPOS* 6 (1926), pp. 75-102. J. A. Montgomery, "Two Notes on the Kalamu Inscription," *JBL* 47 (1928), pp. 196-197. A. Poebel, *Das appositionell bestimmte Pronomen der 1. Pers. Sing. in den westsemitischen Inschriften und im Alten Testament*, Chicago, 1932, pp. 33-43. A. Alt, "Eine syrische Bevölkerungsklasse in ramessidischen Aegypten," *Zeitschrift für Ägyptische Sprache und Altertumskunde* 75 (1930), pp. 16-20.

[3] *A Grammar of the Phoenician Language*, pp. 17-19. See also his *Development of the Canaanite Dialects*, New Haven, 1939, p. 25.

[4] I. e., Akkadian, Ugaritic, transcriptions in classical languages, and Canaanite words in the Amarna texts.

[5] For a discussion of the 9th century inscriptions from Cyprus and Nora, see W. F. Albright, "New Light on the Early History of Phoenician Colonization," *BASOR* #83 (1941), pp. 14-22.

A detailed study of the orthography of the newly discovered Karatepe Inscriptions (late 8th century B. C.) does not fall within the scope of this work, since Hebrew orthography had long since departed from the Phoenician pattern at the time of these inscriptions. In any case the orthography of the Karatepe Inscriptions agrees precisely with the phonetic consonantism of the earlier Phoenician inscriptions. Certain important details of orthography, clarifying obscure grammatical and morphological points in Phoenician, come out of a study of the inscriptions and these are referred to in the notes. For bibliography, see the most recent treatments: A. M. Honeyman, "Epigraphic Discoveries at Karatepe," *PEQ* 81 (1949), pp. 21-39. C. H. Gordon, "Azitawadd's Phoenician Inscription," *JNES* VIII (1949), pp. 108-115. R. Marcus and I. J. Gelb, "The Phoenician Stele Inscription from Cilicia," *JNES* VIII (1949), pp. 116-120. J. Obermann,

The Bronze Spatula Inscription:

1. *mgštk*, "thy offering" (cp. Ugar. *mgṯ*). The form is probably feminine singular with the suffix of the second person masculine singular, -*kā*. See No. 3.

2. *'lk*, "upon thee," to be read *'alêkā*. The contracted diphthong (*ay* > *ê*) is not represented in the orthography.

3. *mgšt*, "my offering." The suffix is required by the context. It was pronounced -*ī* (not indicated in the orthography).[7]

4. *ly*, "to me," **liyā* (cp. Ugar. *ly*).[8] The final vowel (the *ā̆* of the suffix) must have been *anceps* originally. In cases where the vowel was regarded as long, it was retained after the loss of short final vowels in Canaanite. A number of these doublets (in which the final vowel is preserved as long, or dropped if short) occur in the Northwest Semitic languages, often in the same dialect. Examples may be found in the different forms of the singular pronominal suffixes: 2nd masc. -*kā* and -*k* (both occur in Hebrew; the short form is regular in Aramaic); 2nd fem. -*kī* and -*k* (both occur in Hebrew); 3rd masc., -*hū* and -*h* (the long form in Hebrew, the short form in Aramaic). There is a similar development in the treatment of the 2nd sing. perfect of the verb: masc., -*tā* and -*t* (in Hebrew[9] and Aramaic); fem., -*tī* and -*t* (in Hebrew). For the first person sing. we have -*tî* and -*t* (the longer form in Hebrew, Phoenician and Moabite, the shorter in Aramaic).[10]

The Aḥiram Sarcophagus Inscription:

5. *z*, "which" = Hebrew *zū* or possibly *zē*, early Aramaic *zī*, later

New Discoveries at Karatepe, The Connecticut Academy of Arts and Sciences, New Haven, 1949. R. T. O'Callaghan, "The Phoenician Inscription on the King's Statue at Karatepe," *CBQ* XI (1949), pp. 233-248.

[6] See Chapter II.

[7] If the noun were plural (so Albright, "The Phoenician Inscriptions of the Tenth Century B.C. from Byblus," p. 158, and "The Copper Spatula of Byblus and Proverbs 18: 18," *BASOR* # 90 (1943), p. 36 n. 9) we would expect the form of the first person suffix to be -*ay* (as in Hebrew), and this would be represented in the orthography by *yodh*. That this form of the suffix regularly is attached to feminine plurals is attested by such forms as *wšntw* (No. 16) and *'dtw* (No. 20). Cp. also *rbty* to be vocalized *rabbōtay*, following Albright, in the Yeḥawmilk Inscription (line 3).

[8] Cf. C. H. Gordon, *Ugaritic Handbook*, Rome, 1947, I, § 6.16.

[9] The evidence of the Dead Sea Isaiah scroll, as well as the Greek transcriptions in the second column of the Hexapla shows that both forms were read in the biblical text. See note 10.

[10] For a detailed discussion of these forms, and a general analysis of the "long" and "short" forms in Hebrew, see Chapter IV.

Aramaic *dī*, Arabic *ḏū*, *ḏī*, Ugar. *d*. This is normal spelling for the relative and demonstrative in Phoenician.[11]

6. *'bh*, "his father," to be read **'abīhū*. In later Phoenician, the 3rd sing. suffix was indicated by *yodh* instead of *he*, to be read *-iyū* or *-eyū*, the shift *he* to *yodh* being due to palatalization.[12]

7. *w'l*, "and if," to be compared with Hebrew *'ūlay*.[13] If this is correct we may assume the normal Phoenician contraction, *ay* > *ê*. The final vowel would not be represented in the orthography.

8. *'ly*, the Qal perfect 3rd masc. sing. = Hebrew *'ālā*. This appears as a dialectal form in early Phoenician, and is to be vocalized **'alay*. The preservation of the diphthong was due to the presence of final short *a* (*'alaya*) during the period of general diphthong contraction in Canaanite. Later the final short vowel was dropped, along with verbal and case endings, leaving the diphthong.[14] For other similar forms, note No. 12, *bny*, and No. 13, *ḥwy*. In later Phoenician inscriptions, we find forms such as *bn*, "he built," and *ḥz*, "he saw," which follow the regular Hebrew pattern, **banaya* > *bānā*.

9. *wygl*, "and he exposes." Albright has noted correctly that this is a typical *waw* conversive with the imperfect following the perfect *'ly*.[15] If we suppose the same development as in Hebrew, the word should be vocalized *way-yígĕl* (*yígĕl* < *yiglê* < **yiglay*). Compare also the contracted form *ymḥ*, "let him efface" (apparently jussive).

10. *mšpṭh*, "of his authority." Vocalize **mišpaṭihū* (cp. No. 6). Compare also other forms with the 3rd m. s. suffix, *mlkh*, "his kingship," and *sprh*, "his inscription."

The Inscription of Yeḥimilk:

11. *bt* (line 1), "house"; read **bêt* < *bayt*. The form may be construct before *z* here. The contracted diphthong is not represented in the orthography, a clear example of the dominance of the phonetic principle as against historical spelling.

12. *bny* (1), "he built." The same word occurs in Shipiṭbaal (1). See the discussion of this form under No. 8.

[11] See especially J. Friedrich, "Zur Einleitungsformel der ältesten phönizischen Inschriften aus Byblos," *Mélanges Dussaud*, Paris, 1939, pp. 39-47.

[12] Cp. Harris' latest position, *Development of the Canaanite Dialects*, p. 54, and below, note 33.

[13] Cf. Albright, "The Phoenician Inscriptions of the Tenth Century B. C. from Byblus," pp. 155-156, n. 23.

[14] *Ibid.*, p. 155, n. 20.

[15] *Ibid.*, p. 156, n. 24.

13. *ḥwy* (2), "he restored." Vocalize **ḥawway*, following Albright. Cf. No. 8.

14. *šmm* (3), "heavens," **šamêm* for older **šamaym* (Hebrew *šāmáyim*).

15. *'l* (4), "the gods of." Read **'ēlê*, construct plural, as shown by the plural adjective, *qdšm*. The final diphthong is contracted, and therefore not represented. Cf. *'l* (7).

16. *wšntw* (5), "and his years." Vocalize **šanōtêw* < **šanātêhū* < **šanātayhū*. The 3rd m. s. suffix attached to plural nouns seems also to have been *-*êhū* in Ugaritic. In Hebrew we find both -*êhū*,[16] and *-*êw*,[17] for this suffix.

17. *k* (6), "for" = Hebrew *kī*. It is also possible to read *k* "as, like" = Heb. *k*ᵉ,[18] but note the parallel passage in the inscription of Yeḥawmilk (9): *kmlk ṣdq h'* where *kī* is to be read. The only difference between the passages is the omission of the copula, which is to be understood in the Yeḥimilk inscription.

18. *lpn* (7), "before," = Hebrew *lipnê*.

The Inscription of Abibaal:

19. *bm⌈ṣ⌉rm*, "from Egypt" = Hebrew *mimmiṣráyim*. The preposition *b* in Phoenician has the meaning "from," as in Ugaritic and early Hebrew poetry.[19]

The Inscription of Elibaal:

20. *'dtw*, "his lady." Vocalize **'adōttêw*. The form is the so-called plural of majesty.[20]

The Inscription of 'Abda':

21. *bklby*, "son of Kalbai." The adjectival ending *ay* is preserved as a diphthong. Albright has called attention to the same name in Ugaritic.[21] Compare the name *'ky* on the Ruweiseh Arrowhead.[22]

The Kilamuwa Inscription:

22. *'nk* (1), "I" = Heb. *'ānōkî*. Later Phoenician (Punic) shows

[16] See the forms listed in *G–K*, § 91, 1.

[17] See the discussion of this vocalization in Chapter IV, especially the notes on the Gezer Calendar.

[18] So Albright, "The Phoenician Inscriptions of the Tenth Century B. C.," pp. 156-157.

[19] *Ibid.*, p. 158, n. 42.

[20] *Ibid.*, p. 157, n. 41.

[21] *Ibid.*, p. 158, n. 45, and references cited there.

[22] For bibliography, see the Introduction, note 38.

that the final vowel unquestionably was pronounced, although the short form turns up in neo-Punic; cp. Amarna, *a-nu-ki.*

23. *klmw* (1), "Kilamuwa," later pronounced Kilamū.[23] In the Panammu II Inscription, the word also is written *klmw*; according to the orthography of that inscription, it must be vocalized without the final syllable, Kilamū. At the same time, Assyrian transliterations give for the name *pnmw,* the vocalization *pa-na-am-mu-u.*[24]

24. *y'dy* (2). There is no evidence for the vocalization of this word.[25]

25. *'b* (3), "my father," as the context shows. Read **'abî.* Cp. No. 30.

26. *'ḥ* (3), "my brother," **'aḥî.* Contrary to Lidzbarski, a reading, "his brother," is not permissible. The latter would appear as *'ḥy* in the orthography of this period. Cf. No. 32, and note 33.

27. *p'lt* (5), "I did (made)." Read **pa'altî*; this is the standard vocalization of such forms in the Amarna Canaanitisms.

28. *p'l* (5), "they did." Read **pa'alū,* plural, since it is construed with *hlpnyhm,* which must be plural (cp. line 10).

29. *hlpnyhm* (5) and *hlpnym* (10) have proved a puzzle to scholars in the past. The suggestions of Lidzbarski,[26] Torrey,[27] Montgomery,[28] and Friedrich,[29] all are beset with serious difficulties, and involve morphological or orthographic anomalies. Poebel's analysis, on the other hand, commends itself, particularly in the light of more precise knowledge of Phoenician orthography, and parallel syntactical formations.[30] He explains the form *hlpnyhm* as a relative clause, "those who were before me," breaking down the expression into *h,* used as a relative particle, *lpny,* the preposition with the 1st sing. suffix, and *hm,* the 3rd masc. pl. pronominal element used as subject (and copula). The phrase may be vocalized: **ha-lapanay-him.* Such a formation is perfectly proper in Northwest Semitic. In fact this expression is simply an abbreviation for the fuller formula found in the inscription of Azitawadd

[23] Cf. J. Friedrich, "Der Schwund kurzer Endvokale im Nordwestsemitischen," *Zeitschrift für Semitistik* I (1922), p. 5, and Albright, "Notes on Early Hebrew and Aramaic Epigraphy," p. 84.

[24] See the Appendix for discussion of the special problems connected with the orthography of the Panammu Inscriptions.

[25] Friedrich, "Der Schwund kurzer Endvokale im Nordwestsemitischen," p. 5, and D. D. Luckenbill, "Azariah of Judah," *AJSL* XLI (1924-25), pp. 222 ff.

[26] *Ephemeris,* III, p. 227.

[27] "The Zakar and Kalamu Inscriptions," p. 366.

[28] "Two Notes on the Kalamu Inscription," p. 196 f.

[29] "Der Schwund kurzer Endvokale im Nordwestsemitischen," p. 6 n. 1.

[30] A. Poebel, *Das appositionell bestimmte Pronomen der 1. Pers. sing.,* p. 34, n. 4.

B: I: 19, *hmlkm 'š kn lpny*. Poebel regards the form in l. 10 *hlpnym*, as an orthographic error. This, however, may not be the case. The shorter spelling may reflect the more colloquial pronunciation in which the *he* of the pronominal element was palatalized as regularly was the case with pronominal suffixes. In other words, the spelling may reflect a pronunciation **ha-lapanay-yim*, or the like.

30. *bt 'by* (5), "the house of my father." Read probably, **bêt 'abīyă* (Cp. Nos. 4 and 25). As Harris[31] and others have pointed out, the *yodh* of the 1st sing. suffix normally is retained in the spelling when the noun is in the oblique cases, as in Ugaritic. In later Phoenician, the indication of the suffix by *yodh* was extended to nouns in the nominative case as well.[32] See below No. 32, and note 33.

31. *wkt* (6), "and I was." Read **kattî*. The same word occurs again in (10) and (11).

32. *yd* (6), "his(?) hand." Cf. No. 53. The present context and the Hebrew idiom suggest that the suffix is to be read. Vocalize *yadô*.[33]

33. *'ly* (7), "against me"; vocalize **'alay* or **'alayyă*.

34. *d⌈n⌉nym* (7), "the Dananians," a now well-known people of Cilicia.[34] The ending is to be read *-iyyīm*.

35. *'ly* (8), "against him." Read probably **'alêyū* for older **'alêhū*. As in Hebrew the pronominal suffix is attached to the preposition *'al* on the analogy of the plural noun.

36. *bš* (8), "for a sheep." Cp. Hebrew *śē*, Ugar. *š*. The word occurs again in (11).

37. *swt* (8), "garment" (?). The Hebrew cognate *swth* (Gen. 49: 11) is uncertain (cp. Samaritan *kswth*), and the vocalization almost certainly is wrong. Phoenician *swt*[35] and Hebrew *maswē* show that the *waw* is consonantal.

38. *yšbt* (9), "I sat," **yašabtî*.

[31] *A Grammar of the Phoenician Language*, p. 48.

[32] *Ibid.*, p. 48, and Gordon, *Ugaritic Handbook*, I, § 6.16. Cp. Albright, "A Hebrew Letter from the Twelfth Century B. C.," *BASOR* # 73 (1939), p. 12, n. 18. Note, however, in the Yeḥawmilk Inscription, line 8, *šm' ql* ("she heard my voice").

[33] For this form of the suffix in Phoenician, see the discussion of the writers, "The Pronominal Suffixes of the Third Person Singular in Phoenician," *JNES* X (1951), pp. 228-230.

[34] The name, Dananians, occurs a number of times in the Karatepe Inscriptions.

[35] The word occurs in the Batna'm Inscription, line 2. Cf. M. Dunand, "Inscription phénicienne de Byblos," *Kêmi* IV (1931-33), pp. 151-156, and J. Friedrich, "Eine phönizische Inschrift späterer Zeit aus Byblos," *OLZ* 38 (1935), pp. 348-350.

39. *lpn* (9) and *pn* (11), cf. No. 18.

40. *ytlwn* (10), "they writhed"; not *ytl⌜k⌝n* as Lidzbarski and others emended.[36] The form was interpreted correctly by Friedrich as a (h)ithpaʿʿal imperfect indicative, and vocalized, **yitlawwūn*.[37] The meaning in this context has been clarified by Albright.[38]

41. *my* (10 bis, 11 ter, 12, 13, 15), "whoever"; *lmy . . . lmy*, etc., "to some . . . to others." It is to be read **miyă*. Cp. Ugar. *my*, "who," and Amarna Canaanite *miya*.

42. *ḥz* (11, 12), "he saw" = Hebrew *ḥzh*. See the discussion under No. 8.

43. *šty* (11 bis), "I established him." Read **šattīyū* or the like.

44. *lmnʿry* (12), "from his youth"; cp. Heb. *mnʿryw* (Gen. 8:21, etc.). This is the regular form of the suffix following the plural construct of the noun.

45. *wbymy* (12), "but in my days." The 1st person suffix attached to plural nouns is represented by *yodh*: **-ay* or **-ayyă*.

46. *ksy* (12), "[byssus] covered him." The form is the Piel perfect 3rd m. s. with the 3rd m. s. suffix, following Lidzbarski,[39] and Friedrich.[40] Vocalize either **kissāyū* or **kissayyū* < **kissayhū*, following Friedrich.[41] Harris[42] interprets the form as a Pual without the suffix, but the spelling with the final *yodh* in this dialect is highly improbable. Cf. Nos. 8 and 42.

47. *tmkt* (13), "I grasped," **tamaktî*.

48. *št* (13), "they set," **šātū*, not **šōt* or the like. This is not the infinitive (absolute) construction with the pronoun, now familiar from the Azitawadd and later inscriptions. In that construction, the pronoun regularly follows the verbal form (e. g. *wškr ʾnk . . .* lines 7-8); when the pronoun precedes, as here, a finite form of the verb follows.

49. *bbny* (13/14), "of (from among) my sons." Read **babanay* or the like.

50. *tḥtn* (14), "in my place." Vocalize, as in Hebrew, *taḥtēnî*.

51. *ykbd* (14, 15), "may they [not] give honor to." Vocalize

[36] *Ephemeris* III, p. 223; C. C. Torrey, "The Zakar and Kalamu Inscriptions," pp. 367 f.

[37] "Der Schwund kurzer Endvokale," p. 6, n. 2.

[38] "Notes on Early Hebrew and Aramaic Epigraphy," pp. 84-85.

[39] *Ephemeris* III, pp. 237-238.

[40] "Der Schwund kurzer Endvokale," p. 5.

[41] *Ibid.*, pp. 5-6.

[42] *Phoenician Grammar*, p. 42 and n. 17, where, however, he misinterprets the passage: the subject would not be "he," but "it," "byssus."

*yakabbidū or the like. The context requires the plural form. Cp. Amarna *ia-ka-bi-id* (= *yakabbid*).

52. *bsprz* (14) and *hsprz* (15), "(in) this inscription." For *z* cf. No. 5.

53. *r'š* (15, 16), "his (?) head." Vocalize **rōšô*. On the reading *rōš* for head, compare Amarna *ru-šu-nu* ("our head"). In connection with the suffix and the interpretation of the phrase, see note 33.

54. *bt* (16), "house." The word is in the absolute state, indicating that the contraction of the diphthong was general, and not as in the Hebrew of the Massoretic text: *báyit,* absolute, *bêt,* construct.

The preceding analysis is sufficient to show that the Phoenician orthography of the 10th–9th centuries followed rigorously consonantal principles. No forms occur in which it is necessary or probable to suppose the presence of *matres lectionis* in the final position, much less medially.

We may briefly summarize the evidence as follows. For forms in which final vowels undoubtedly were pronounced in Phoenician, but are not represented in the orthography, see Nos. 1, 2, 3, 4, 5, 6, 7, 10, 15, 17, 18, 22, 23, 25, 26, 27, 28, 30, 31, 32 (?), 35, 36, 38, 39, 41, 42, 43, 44, 46, 47, 48, 50, 51, 52, and 53 (?).

Contracted diphthongs are not indicated in the spelling as they would be if the orthography were historical, or if *matres lectionis* were in use.[43] Examples of contraction in the medial position are Nos. 2, 11, 14, 16, 19, 20, 30, 35, 44, and 54. In the final position, where historical spelling might be expected, the evidence, while limited, agrees with the preceding material: Nos. 7 (?), 9 (?), 15, 18, 32 (?), 36, 39, and 53 (?).

On the other hand, diphthongs which were formed after the period of the general contraction in the Bronze Age, are represented by the consonantal element in the diphthong. Such diphthongs appeared, primarily, when final short vowels were dropped (at the beginning of the Iron Age) leaving a diphthongal cluster in the final position, i. e. a semivowel preceded by a heterogeneous vowel, and sporadically when final long vowels were lost, leaving the same situation. It is to be noted also that diphthongs regularly were preserved when, in given forms, the semivocalic element was doubled (**ayyă* > **ayy* > *ay*). The diphthongs represented in the early Phoenician texts all fall into these categories: Nos. 8, 12, 13, 21, 29, 33, 45, and 49.

The most striking features of early Phoenician orthography are the absence of historical spelling and the flexibility in spelling practice. There is practically no evidence at all for the preservation of older

[43] The diphthongs referred to are *aw* and *ay,* unless otherwise specified.

spellings. On the contrary, there was regular and frequent revision of the orthography to conform to changes in morphology and phonology.[44] This flexibility must be attributed to the operation of a strong phonemic principle. The Phoenician alphabet was a simple, practicable set of phonemic symbols which lent itself readily to phonetic writing. Its rapid spread and wide usage among other dialects and languages amply illustrate the phonetic adaptability of the script. As suggested by Harris,[45] the phonemic character of the alphabet and the absence of a highly centralized scribal caste prevented the development of a stereotyped orthographic tradition.

The principle of phonetic consonantism spread with the Phoenician alphabet. In the Semitic dialects which borrowed the alphabet, the signs were used, initially at least, to represent consonantal phonemes. In the earliest phase, no *matres lectionis* would appear in the orthography. This point is particularly pertinent to the discussion of Aramaic orthography, and will be developed in the next chapter.

[44] All forms are most easily explained as current in the local speech. The only reservation to be made is that the language of the inscriptions may represent the formal or elegant pronunciation as against the colloquial. The flexibility of Phoenician writing, as well as of other Canaanite dialects and Aramaic, has not generally been recognized.

[45] *Development of the Canaanite Dialects*, p. 25. Standardized formulas naturally are met with in almost all royal inscriptions, but the orthography is affected only in the rarest instances. In the late Byblian inscriptions, there was a deliberate effort to reproduce not only the content but the orthography of the earlier royal inscriptions (but even in these later linguistic changes are reflected in the orthography). Cf. Albright, "The Phoenician Inscriptions of the Tenth Century B.C.," pp. 159-160.

CHAPTER II

EARLY ARAMAIC ORTHOGRAPHY

OLD ARAMAIC [1] was, for all practical purposes, an unknown language before the end of the 19th century. Then several inscriptions were discovered at Zinčirli: the Panammu II inscription in 1888, the Panammu I in 1890,[2] and the Bir-RKB in 1891; [3] and at Nerab: the inscriptions of Sin-zer-ibni and Agbar in 1891.[4] In 1898, F. E. Peiser published the enigmatic inscription on a stele from Ördek-burnu.[5] And in 1908, H. Pognon published the important Zakir Stele, which he had previously discovered.[6]

[1] I. e., the language of the Aramaeans in Syria during the period of these inscriptions: from the tenth to the seventh centuries B. C.

[2] The standard edition of these inscriptions is E. Sachau, "Die Inschrift des Königs Panammū von Šam/al," Ch. IV in *Ausgrabungen in Sendschirli*, I, *Einleitung und Inschriften*, Berlin, 1893, pp. 62-84, and Plates VI-VIII. For the earlier bibliography, see Lidzbarski, *Handbuch der nordsemitischen Epigraphik*, Weimar, 1898, I (Text), pp. 440-443 (references), and G. A. Cooke, *A Text-Book of North-Semitic Inscriptions*, Oxford, 1903, pp. 159-180. For more recent literature, see F. Rosenthal, *Die aramaistische Forschung*, Leiden, 1939, Chs. 1, 2; also H. L. Ginsberg's review article of this work, "Aramaic Studies Today," *JAOS* 62 (1942), pp. 233 ff.

[3] We follow the usual procedure in designating as Panammu I the so-called "Hadadinschrift" of Panammu I, and as Panammu II, the "Panammuinschrift" of Bir-RKB; while Bir-RKB stands for the "Bauinschrift" of the same king. The standard treatments of the Bir-RKB Inscription are those of Lidzbarski, *Handbuch der nordsemitischen Epigraphik*, I, pp. 443-444, II (Plates), No. XXIV, and Cooke, *op. cit.*, pp. 180-185. For bibliography, see note 2.

[4] Cf. Lidzbarski, *Handbuch*, I, p. 445, II, Plate XXV; Cooke, *op. cit.*, pp. 186-191. It was not considered necessary to deal with these inscriptions in detail, since they fall at the very end of the period with which we are concerned, and in any case only confirm the orthographic principles established on the basis of the other inscriptions.

[5] *OLZ* I (1898), cols. 5-8. The standard edition of this text is F. v. Luschan, *Ausgrabungen in Sendschirli*, IV, Berlin, 1911, p. 328; facsimile, p. 239. The text is very obscure, and attempts at translation have been uniformly unsuccessful. Needless to say it cannot be used for orthographic analysis. For a discussion of the difficulties, see Lidzbarski, *Ephemeris für semitische Epigraphik*, III, pp. 192-206, and Plates XIII-XV. For bibliography, see J. Friedrich, *Kleinasiatische Sprachdenkmäler*, Berlin, 1932, p. 39.

[6] H. Pognon, *Inscriptions sémitique de la Syrie, de la Mésopotamie, et de la région de Mossoul*, Paris, 1907-1908, pp. 156-178, Plates IX, X, XXXV, XXXVI. Lidzbarski deals with the inscription in his *Ephemeris*, III, pp. 1-11. In addition to the bibliography given by Lidzbarski, note the following: C. C. Torrey, "The

Because of its affinities with contemporary Canaanite, and its considerable divergences from later Aramaic, the language of these inscriptions was regarded by most scholars as an artificial mixture of some kind.[7] The two Panammu Inscriptions, moreover, presented so many special problems in orthography and morphology when compared with the other inscriptions, that it became necessary to suppose a separate Zinčirli dialect.[8]

With the discoveries of more recent years, sufficient data accumulated to classify the language of the inscriptions as Old Aramaic. In 1931, Ronzevalle published the long inscription on the Sujin Stele;[9] it proved to be in the same language as Bir-RKB and Zakir. In the same year, the Hazael Inscription from Arslan-Tash appeared.[10] In 1940, Friedrich published an Old Aramaic Inscription from Tell Halaf (Gozan),[11] and

Zakar and Kalamu Inscriptions," *JAOS* 35 (1915-17), pp. 353-364. W. F. Albright, "Notes on Early Hebrew and Aramaic Epigraphy," *JPOS* 6 (1926), pp. 85-88. M. Noth, "La'asch und Hazrak," *ZDPV* 52 (1929), pp. 124-141. H. L. Ginsberg, "Aramaic Dialect Problems," *AJSL* 50 (1933), pp. 1-9.

[7] Cf. Lidzbarski, *Ephemeris* III, pp. 2-3. For the latest discussion of the language of the inscriptions, see Rosenthal, *op. cit.*, pp. 46 ff., Ginsberg, "Aramaic Studies Today," pp. 233 ff., and R. A. Bowman, "Aramaeans, Aramaic, and the Bible," *JNES* VII (1948), especially pp. 71-73.

[8] The Panammu Inscriptions are dealt with in a special Appendix. Neither the language nor the orthography of these inscriptions corresponds to the standard practice of the Old Aramaic inscriptions, the Meša' Stone, or the pre-exilic Hebrew inscriptions. While these peculiarities deserve attention, they seem to have been limited to the region of Zinčirli, and in any case do not directly affect the evolution of Hebrew orthography.

[9] S. Ronzevalle, "Fragments d'inscriptions araméenes des environs d'Alep," *Mélanges de l'Université Saint-Joseph*, XV (1930-1931), pp. 237-260, Plates XXXII-XLV. The literature on this inscription is very scanty: J. Cantineau, "Remarques sur la stèle araméene de Sefiré-Soudjin," *Revue d'Assyriologie* 28 (1931), pp. 167-178. H. Bauer, "Ein aramäischer Staatsvertrag aus dem 8. Jahrhundert v. Chr. Die Inschrift der Stele von Sudschin," *AfO* VIII (1932), pp. 1-16. G. R. Driver, "Notes on the Aramaic Inscription from Soudschin," *AfO* VIII (1933), pp. 203-206. J. Friedrich and B. Landsberger, "Zu der altaramäischen Stele von Sudschin," *ZA* N. F. 7 (1933), pp. 313-318. J. Friedrich, "Kein König פלמה in der Stele von Sudschin," *ZA* N. F. 9 (1936), pp. 327-328.

[10] The official publication is Thureau-Dangin, Barrois, Dossin and Dunand, *Arslan-Tash*, Paris, 1931, *Text* pp. 135-138, *Atlas*, Plate XLVII, p. 112a. This inscription belongs to the latter half of the ninth century. Its script is less archaic than that of the Bir-Hadad stele, and therefore the date of the latter is fixed around the middle of the ninth century. The only form of orthographic interest in this fragment is *mr'n*, "our lord," **mar'an*. On the loss of the final *a* of the suffix, see No. 26.

[11] Friedrich, Meyer, Ungnad and Weidner, *Die Inschriften vom Tell Halaf*, Berlin, 1940, pp. 68-70 and Plate 29. R. A. Bowman, "The Old Aramaic Alphabet at Tell Halaf," *AJSL* 58 (1941), pp. 359-367. W. F. Albright, "A Votive Stele

Ingholt published a number of graffiti found at Hamath.[12] About the same time, the Bir-Hadad Inscription came to light.[13]

The present study deals principally with the orthography of the Old Aramaic inscriptions.[14] A special section is devoted to the peculiarities of the Panammu Inscriptions.[15] The texts will be treated in chronological order: the Old Aramaic Inscription from Tell Halaf (ca. 900 B. C.),[16] the Bir-Hadad Stele (ca. 850 B. C.), the Zakir Stele (ca. 800-775 B. C.), the Sujin Stele (ca. 750 B. C.), and the Bir-RKB Inscription (ca. 730 B. C.).[17]

The Tell Halaf Inscription:

This fragment, which apparently is the oldest known Aramaic inscription,[18] has not adequately been deciphered. One word is clear, however, and important for orthographic purposes.

1. *zy*. Both the *zayin* and the *yodh* are certain, and the word is marked off by vertical strokes. There can be no doubt that it is the characteristic Aramaic relative, spelled as always in the early period with *z* (much later, it was written with *d*). The original interdental

Erected by Ben-Hadad I of Damascus to the God Melcarth," *BASOR* # 87 (1942), p. 25 n. 3.

[12] H. Ingholt, *Rapport préliminaire sur sept campagnes de fouilles à Hama en Syrie (1932-1938)*, Copenhagen, 1940, pp. 115 ff. and Plate XXXIX. There is one fairly clear word of interest in graffite No. 1, *⌜b⌝yt*, "house of," **bayt*. The diphthong was not contracted, even though the noun is in the construct state; cf. No. 40. These graffiti date from the tenth to the eighth centuries B. C.

[13] This inscription was first published by M. Dunand, " Stèle araméene dédiée à Melqart," *Bulletin du Musée de Beyrouth* III, pp. 65-76. W. F. Albright, " A Votive Stele Erected by Ben-Hadad I of Damascus to the God Melcarth," pp. 23-29. G. Levi Della Vida and W. F. Albright, " Some Notes on the Stele of Ben-Hadad," *BASOR* # 90 (1943), pp. 30-34. M. Dunand, " A propos de la stèle de Melqart du musée d'Alep," *Bulletin du Musée de Beyrouth* VI (1946), pp. 41-45.

[14] We restrict the study to words and forms which are relatively clear, in order to establish validly the principles of orthography. Later, it may be possible on the basis of the orthographic analysis to resolve obscurities and even restore illegible texts.

[15] The material is presented in the Appendix. See note 8.

[16] Because of its fragmentary nature, it is very difficult to date this inscription accurately. There is considerable disagreement among the scholars. Bowman holds to a date in the 8th century, while Albright fixes it in the early part of the 9th (for references see note 11).

[17] The dates for these inscriptions are fixed on epigraphic grounds, and are universally accepted. In the case of Bir-Hadad and Bir-RKB there are also historical controls.

[18] See note 16.

spirant (*ḏ*) was still pronounced.[19] The *yodh* is a *mater lectionis*. This form (also in Bir-Hadad lines 1 and 4) gives evidence that final vowel letters were in use in Aramaic by the end of the tenth century B. C.

The Bir-Hadad Inscription:

As already noted, the word *zy* occurs twice in this inscription. Otherwise, there are no forms with vowel letters, either in final or medial position. Some words require attention, nevertheless:

2. *nṣb'* (1), "the stele." The article is indicated by *aleph*, which is of course consonantal. As will be seen, there is no evidence for the early quiescing of *aleph* in Aramaic.[20] Cf. *nṣb'* in Zakir (1).

3. *lmr'h* (3), "to his lord." Read **mar'eh*, with the regular Aramaic 3rd m. s. suffix, *-eh*. Cp. *lh* (4) and No. 4.

4. *lqlh* (4/5), "to his voice." Read **laqāleh* or the like, not **laqôleh* (< **qawl*). There is no evidence for the contraction of diphthongs, *ay* and *aw*, in Old Aramaic under any circumstances. The form here is equivalent to Biblical Aramaic *qāl*, Syriac *qālâ*, Ethiopic *qāl*, Arabic *qāl* (along with *qawl*), and South Arabic *ql* (i. e. *qāl*). Compare the metaplastic forms in South Arabic, *yawm* and *yām*, "day."[21]

The Zakir Stele:

5. *'lwr* (A: 1), "Iluwer"; the pronunciation is based on Akkadian transcriptions.[22]

6. *'nh* (A: 2), "[I am] a humble man." Read **'ānē* (< *'āniy*) or **'ᵃnē* (< *'anīy*). The *he* is used here as a *mater lectionis* to represent final *ē*.[23]

7. *'nh* (A: 2, etc.), "I," Biblical Aramaic *'ᵃnā*. The *he* is used here to represent final *ā*.

[19] That proto-Semitic *ṯ* (ث), *ḏ* (ذ), *ẓ̱* (ظ), and *ḍ* (ض), were preserved in the pronunciation of Old Aramaic, was first pointed out by D. H. Müller, "Die altsemitischen Inschriften von Sendschirli," *Wiener Zeitschrift für die Kunde des Morgenlandes* VII (1893), pp. 113 ff.

[20] Later, when *aleph* quiesced generally in the final position, it was pressed into service as a *mater lectionis*. In Syriac, it completely displaced *he* as a vowel letter. On the peculiar use of *aleph* in the Panammu Inscriptions, see the Appendix.

[21] Cf. Ginsberg, "על תעודות לכיש," *BJPES* III (1935), p. 79. The point will be discussed further in the section on Hebrew orthography.

[22] Cf. W. F. Albright, "Notes on Early Hebrew and Aramaic Epigraphy," p. 87.

[23] In the phrase *'š 'nh*, *'š* is to be read "man." The word occurs regularly in Old Aramaic, and the Elephantine papyri. On the expression in the text, cp. Num. 12: 3!

8. *b'l šmyn* (A: 3), "Ba'al šamayn" = Canaanite *Ba'al šamêm.* In Aramaic, the diphthong was not contracted and is therefore indicated in the orthography.

9. *'my* (A: 3), "with me, at my side," **'immî.* The *yodh* is used here as a vowel letter for final *î*.

10. *whmlkny* (A: 3), "and he caused me to rule." The regular causative in Old Aramaic is the *haphel,* as in Biblical Aramaic. The *yodh* is used as a vowel letter.

11. *whwḥd* (A: 4), "and he united," **hawḥid.* The diphthong is preserved in the *haphel* of *pe waw* verbs.

12. *mḥnth* (A: 5), "his host," **maḥ^{a}nīteh* or **maḥ^{a}nūteh.* Cf. No. 15. The word occurs frequently in this inscription.

13. *qwh* (A: 6), "Cilicia," Akkadian "Qu-e." The *he* is used as a *mater lectionis.* Cp. Biblical *qwh,* I Kings 10: 28 (bis) = II Chron. 1: 16 (bis).

14. ⌜*h*⌝*mw* (A: 9), "they (?)." The reading is not certain. Vocalize **him(m)ū* or **humū* in this period. The *waw* is used as a vowel letter for final *ū*.

15. *mḥnwt(hm)* (A: 9), "their hosts," **maḥan^{a}wāt*; this is a customary plural formation in nouns with weak third radical.[24]

16. *wśmw* (A: 9), "and they set," **waśāmū.*

17. *mlky' 'l* (A: 9), "these kings." The demonstrative is to be vocalized **'ēl,* as in Ezra 5: 15 (Q^{e}re).[25] Cf. Panammu I, *'mrt 'l* (29), "these words."

18. *hrmw* (A: 10), "they raised," **harīmū.*

19. *h'mqw* (A: 10), "they made deeper." The *waw* is used as a vowel letter to indicate final *ū*.

20. *w'ś'* (A: 11), "and I lifted," **'eśśa'.* The *aleph* is consonantal; *lamedh aleph* verbs had not yet fallen together with verbs *lamedh yodh* and *waw.* The form probably is an imperfect with *waw conversive,* since the context requires a past tense. See the discussion of this passage under No. 22.

21. *ydy* (A: 11), "my hands," **yaday.*

22. *wy'nny* (A: 11), "and he answered me." The diphthong formed in the imperfect of *lamedh yodh* verbs was not contracted in the Aramaic of this period, cf. Nos. 46, 47 and 53. It seems more probable therefore

[24] Cf. C. Brockelmann, *Syrische Grammatik,* Berlin, 1899, § 120, for this development in Syriac.

[25] Cf. Bauer and Leander, *Grammatik des Biblisch-Aramäischen,* Halle, 1927, § 21k.

that we have here a *yaqtil* formation involving syncope of the *yodh* (i. e., **ya'niyinî* > **ya'nīnî* > **ya'nēnî*),[26] rather than a *yaqtal* form, involving contraction of the diphthong (**ya'naynî* > **ya'nênî*).

23. *'ly* (A: 12), "to me," **'ēlay*.

24. *ḥzyn* (A: 12), "seers." Vocalize **ḥāziyīn* or as in Biblical Aramaic, *ḥāzayn* (< **ḥāzayīn*).

25. *ky* (A: 13), "for," **kī*. The word occurs frequently in *Aḥiqar*.[27]

26. *'mk* (A: 14), "with thee," **'immak*. The final *a* of the suffix had already been lost.

27. *mḥ'w* (A: 15), "they struck," i. e., "they laid siege to." Read **maḥa'ū*.

28. *'lyk* (A: 15), "against thee," **'alayk*.

29. *znh* (A: 17, B: 14, 18, 19), "this," **ḏ^e^nā*.

Zakir B:

This part of the inscription is fragmentary but several forms are sufficiently clear to be treated here.

30. *'yt* (B: 5, 11, 15, 16), sign of the accusative = Phoenician *'yt*. Cp. Hebrew *'t*, later Aramaic *yat*, Syriac *l^e^wat*, cf. Panammu I ותה (28), etc.[28] The original form may have been **'awat* or **wat*. This particle, as well as most of the other so-called Canaanite constructions and forms, probably was native to Old Aramaic, which had not yet diverged widely from early Northwest Semitic.[29] While some intermixture between Canaanite and Aramaic during the period of Aramaean invasion and settlement in Syria may have taken place, these inscriptions offer too little evidence of it to warrant the designation, "mixed dialect."

31. *śmth* (B: 6), "I made it (?)." Vocalize **śāmteh* or the like.

32. *bty* (B: 9), "the houses of [the gods]." Read **battay*, as in Syriac. Final *yodh* represents either the diphthong *ay* or the vowel *ī* in all the Old Aramaic inscriptions.

33. *bnyt* (B: 10, Bir-RKB 20), "I built," **banayt* (< **banaytu*). This form, along with Nos. 46, 47 and 53, shows that when the diphthong *ay* was formed in the inflection of *lamedh yodh* verbs, it was not

[26] *Ibid.*, § 6t, x, § 47b.

[27] Cf. A. Cowley, *Aramaic Papyri of the Fifth Century B. C.*, Oxford, 1923, pp. 215 ff. and the index.

[28] Cf. Brockelmann, *Grundriss der vergleichenden Grammatik der semitischen Sprachen*, I (*Laut- und Formenlehre*), Berlin, 1908, § 106 Ce.

[29] See the Appendix *ad loc.*

contracted. Note also that the first person singular verbal afformative in early Aramaic was *-t,* rather than *-tu* or *tī.*

34. *'w* (B: 21), "or," **'aw,* as in Syriac.

The Sujin Stele:

The work of Ronzevalle, Cantineau and Bauer has by no means solved the knotty epigraphic and linguistic problems of the Sujin Stele. A set of clear photographs, an accurate handcopy, and a systematic treatment of the contents are badly needed. The fragmentary and eroded parts of the stele, where readings and word divisions are especially difficult to determine and where the context frequently is uncertain, will not be considered in this treatment. In orthographic analysis it is essential to deal primarily with words which are relatively clear and in an intelligible context.

35. *'dy* (Aa: 1, etc.), "treaties of." Read probably **'ēday* or **'aday.* Cf. No. 32.

36. *bny* (Aa: 2, etc.), "children of," **bānay.*

37. *b'ly* (Aa: 4, etc.), "citizens of," **ba'lay.* Cf. Bir-RKB lines 10, 11.

38. *klh* (Aa: 5), "all of it," **kulleh.*

39. *b[n]wh* (Aa: 5). The reading is difficult. The context has, "and treaties of KTK with Arpad . . . and with all Aram, and with MṢR and with *b[ ]wh* . . ." Bauer has pointed out that the rest of the line is illegible. The reading of this form generally is restored as *b[n]wh,* "his sons," but this hardly makes sense in the context. Perhaps the expression is to be understood as the masculine equivalent of the common Hebrew expression, *b^e^nōtêhā,* "its villages." This reading illustrates the difficulties involved in using the Sujin Stele at the present time. The form cannot well be used for orthographic analysis. Cf. No. 68.

40. *byt* (Aa: 6, Bir-RKB *passim*), "house of." Note that the diphthong is not contracted, though the word is in the construct state: **bayt.*

41. *nb'* (Aa: 8), "Nabu." The *aleph* is consonantal.

42. *ywm* (Aa: 12), "day," **yawm.*

43. *lylh* (Aa: 12), "night," **laylā.* The word is written *llh* in the Meša' Inscription, with apparent contraction of the diphthong.[30] The accusative ending *-ā* (an originally *short* vowel), is indicated by the *he.*

44. ⌈*p*⌉*qḥw* (Aa: 13), "open (imperative)," *p^e^qaḥū.*

45. *'ynykm* (Aa: 13), "your eyes," **'aynaykum.* The dipththong is not contracted before suffixes. Cf. No. 40.

[30] See Chapter III, No. 41.

46. *lḥzy* (Aa: 13), "to see." The reading follows Bauer and Ginsberg.[31] There is now considerable evidence for an early Aramaic infinitive without the preformative *mem*: cf. Panammu I *lbny* and *lnṣb* (10); and *l'mr* regularly in the Elephantine papyri. Vocalize **lahazay* (?).[32]

47. *thry* (Ab: 2), "she shall conceive," **tihray.*

48. *yhynqn* (Ab: 3, 4), "they shall suckle." Vocalize **yᵉhayniqān* or the like. The diphthong is preserved in the *haphel* of verbs *pe yodh.*

49. *'lym* (Ab: 3), "a young one." Vocalize **'ulaym,* a *qutayl* formation.[33] Cp. Talmudic *'wlym.*

50. *ssyh* (Ab: 3), "a mare," **sūsyā.* Cp. Nos. 51 and 54.

51. *šwrh* (Ab: 4), "cow," **ṯawrā.*

52. *š'n* (Ab: 4), "ewes," **ṯa'ān.* Cp. Ugar. *ṯ'at,* and *t't'* in the Elephantine papyri (as suggested by Albright). The standard Aramaic form of the feminine plural absolute is preserved in these inscriptions.[34]

53. *thwy* (Ab: 6), "it shall be." Read **tihway.*

54. *klmh* (Ab: 7 bis), "reproach, humiliation" = Heb. *kᵉlimmā.*

55. *lḥyh* (Ab: 7), "accursed," **laḥyā* or the like. The form is a passive participle. Cp. *lḥy'* from the Elephantine papyri.[35]

56. *'rbh* (Ab: 8), "locust" = Heb. *'arbē*; Ugar. *'irby.* The ending was originally *-iy* > *ē* (in Hebrew and Aramaic).

57. *twl'h* (Ab: 8), "worm" = Heb. *tôlē'ā.* Vocalize **tawli'ā.*

58. *mḥwh* (Ab: 12), "destruction." Read **maḥwā* = Syriac *maḥwā,* a back formation from *maḥwātā.*[36] Cp. Arabic *maḥwat.*

59. *z'* (Ab: 16), "this." The same word occurs in Egyptian Aramaic.[37] Later Aramaic has *d'*. The *aleph* is originally consonantal in this word; and there is no evidence for the use of *aleph* as a *mater lectionis* in this inscription or those of Bir-Hadad, Zakir or Bir-RKB.[38]

[31] Bauer, "Ein aramäischer Staatsvertrag aus dem 8. Jahrhundert v. Chr.," p. 6.

[32] The infinitive of the simple conjugation in Ugar. is also formed from the root consonants, without preformative or afformative.

[33] Cf. Bauer and Leander, *Grammatik des Biblisch-Aramäischen,* § 51 v".

[34] This form, however, does not occur in the Panammu Inscriptions; see discussion in the Appendix.

[35] Cowley, *Aramaic Papyri of the Fifth Century B. C.,* p. 115. The meaning of the word has been clarified by Ginsberg, "A Further Note on the Aramaic Contract published by Bauer and Meissner," *JAOS* 59 (1939), p. 105.

[36] Cf. Brockelmann, *Syrische Grammatik,* § 109e.

[37] Cf. Cowley, *Aramaic Papyri,* references in the index, p. 284.

[38] See note 20.

60. *'ykh* (Ab: 18), "as," **'aykā*. This is the longer form, parallel to *'yk* (Ab: 16, etc.). Both forms appear in Biblical Hebrew.[39]

61. *h'* (Ab: 18), "behold!", *ha'*. The same word occurs commonly in Biblical and Egyptian Aramaic.

62. *bšmyn* (Ba: 7), "in the heavens." Read **bašamayn* or the like.

63. *ḥdh* (Ba: 8), "one" = Biblical Aramaic *ḥ*^{a}*dā*.

64. *kh* (Ca: 1), "thus" = Biblical Aramaic *kā*.

65. *mh* (Ca: 1), "what (?)." Vocalize **mā* or **mah* (Ugar. *mh*). The *he* originally was consonantal but whether or when it lost consonantal force cannot be determined. Cf. Panammu I, 12.

66. *byth* (Cb: 3), "his house," **bayteh*. Cf. No. 40.

67. *mly* (Cb: 4), "the words of," **millay*.

68. *mlwh* (Cb: 5/6), "his words." The form is difficult. The suffix here is to be compared with Syriac *-awhī* and Aramaic *-ôhī*. It differs, however, as to the manner in which the secondary suffix has been added: **ayhū* > **ayū* > *aw*, plus the secondary suffix produces **-awh* or **aweh*. The form can hardly be vocalized **-awhī*, because the final *ī* is regularly indicated by the vowel letter in these texts (i. e. *-why*). Cp. the form of the suffix in Egyptian and Biblical Aramaic, Syriac and Jewish Aramaic. Several other forms seem to fall into the same category: *rbwh* (Ab: 21), "his nobles (?)," *qdmwh* in Nerab II: 2; also see No. 39.

The Bir-RKB Inscription:

This inscription of Bir-RKB, unlike the other (Panammu II), is written in the standard Aramaic of his day. Why an attempt was made to preserve the archaizing practices of his predecessors in one inscription, and abandoned in the other in favor of current usage, is difficult to say.[40] The language of Bir-RKB is identical in all significant respects with that of the earlier Aramaic inscriptions, Bir-Hadad, Zakir and Sujin. That this was the common language of the Aramaeans in Syria from the tenth century B. C. on, whether at Damascus or Hamath or Šam'al, can hardly be doubted.

69. *tgltplysr* (3, 6), "Tiglath-pileser." Cp. *tgltplsr* in Panammu II (13, 15, 16). The *yodh* may be an internal *mater lectionis*, or may represent the diphthong *ay*, resolved from *ê*.[41] The name regularly appears as *tgltpl'sr* in the Old Testament.

[39] See the treatment of this subject in Chapter IV.

[40] See the discussion in the Appendix.

[41] Cf. A. Poebel, *Das appositionell bestimmte Pronomen der 1. Pers. sing.*, pp. 49-50, n. 3. He reads the name as **tugúltapílaysár* in contrast with the representation in the Panammu II Inscription: **tugúltapílêsár*.

70. *rb'y* (4), "the four parts of." Cp. *rb't* in Panammu II (14). The ending is the construct plural, *-ay*.

71. *'by* (4, 7 bis, 12), "my father," **'abî*.

72. *bṣdqy* (4/5), "in my righteousness," **baṣidqî*.

73. *hwšbny* (5), "he caused me to sit," **hawṯibanî*. Cf. Panammu II (19).

74. *mr'y* (5, 6, 9), "my lord," **mar'î*.

75. *rṣt* (8), "I ran." Read *rāẓĕt* or **rāẓt*.

76. *'šwr* (9), "Assur." The *waw* is an internal *mater lectionis* representing *ū*. The same spelling of this word also appears a number of times in Panammu II.

77. *w'ḥzt* (11), "and I took," **wa'aḥaḏt* or the like.

78. *hyṭbth* (12), "I made it better," **hayṭibteh* or the like.

79. *htn'bw* (14), "they coveted (?)." The verb usually is construed as an infixed-*t-n* form. This, however, is not necessary. The root is *n'b*, parallel to *'bh* and *y'b*, and perhaps a secondary formation.[42]

80. *'ḥy* (14), "my colleagues." Cp. the plural form *'yḥ* in the Panammu Inscriptions. Vocalize **'aḥḥay*.

81. *mlky'* (14, 15), "the kings." Read **malkayya'*.

82. *mh* (15), "whatever." Cf. No. 65.[43]

83. *byty* (15), "my house," **baytî*.

84. *byṭb* (16), "a good house" (**bayt ṭāb* > **bayṭ-ṭāb*). The noun is in the absolute state.[44]

85. *lyšh* (16), "it was not," **layṯeh*. Cf. Zakir B (15), *lyš*.

86. *l'bhy* (16), "to my fathers," **la'abāhay*. Cp. plural forms (with suffixes) which are built on masculine stems in Egyptian Aramaic.

87. *mlky* (16/17), "kings of," **malkay*.

88. *h'* (17), "behold!" Cf. No. 61.[45]

89. *klmw* (17/18), "Kilamū." It is now generally agreed that this refers to the former king of *Y'dy*, whose palace the immediate forebears of Bir-RKB possessed. Cf. No. 23 in Chapter I.

90. *ph'* (18, cf. 19), "and it was," **pahū'*.

91. *śtw'* (19), "the winter" (emphatic state), **śitwa'*.

[42] *Ibid.*, p. 51, n. 5.

[43] Cf. Friedrich, "Kein König פלמה in der Stele von Sudschin," p. 328.

[44] The word occurs several times in the Elephantine papyri, Cowley, *Aramaic Papyri*, index p. 279. For a discussion of the form, see Gordon, "The Aramaic Incantation in Cuneiform," *AfO* XII (1939), p. 114.

[45] Cf. Ginsberg, "Aramaic Studies Today," p. 235, n. 31.

92. *kyṣ'* (19), "the summer," **kayẓa'*, Heb. *qyṣ*. Note the dissimilation of the first emphatic as frequently in later Aramaic.[46]

A fixed set of principles governed the orthography of the Old Aramaic inscriptions. The spelling of these inscriptions is characterized by the regular use of *matres lectionis* to indicate final vowels, the absence of medial vowel letters (although this was modified sporadically in the late eighth century in the spelling of foreign words), and the consistent representation of diphthongs by their consonantal element.[47]

The final vowel *ī* is indicated in the orthography by *yodh*: Nos. 1, 9, 10, 22, 25, 71, 72, 73, 74 and 83.

The final vowel *ū* is represented by *waw*: Nos. 14, 16, 18, 19, 27, 44, 79 and 89.

The final vowel *ā* is represented by *he*: Nos. 7, 29, 43, 50, 51, 54, 55, 57, 58, 60, 63, 64, 65? and 82?.

The final vowel *ē* also is represented by *he*: Nos. 6, 13 and 56.

Whereas in Phoenician, most diphthongs were contracted, this did not occur in Old Aramaic. Wherever the diphthongs *ay* and *aw* are expected on the basis of etymology or the evidence of cognate languages, they are indicated in the orthography.

The diphthong *ay* is represented by *yodh*: Nos. 8, 17, 21, 23, 24?, 28, 30, 32, 33, 35, 36, 37, 40, 43, 45, 46, 47, 48, 49, 53, 60, 62, 66, 67, 69?, 70, 78, 80, 81, 83, 84, 85, 86, 87 and 92.

The diphthong *aw* is represented by *waw*: Nos. 11, 34, 39?, 42, 51, 57, 68? and 73.

When the Aramaeans borrowed the Phoenician alphabet, they naturally adapted it to the peculiarities of their own language. As already indicated, they used certain alphabetic signs to represent not only their normal Phoenician value, but also other closely related phonemes, which were no longer preserved in Phoenician. They also modified the principle of phonetic consonantism to the extent of using consonantal signs to indicate final vowels. The latter change must have taken place almost immediately after the adoption of the Phoenician alphabet. The borrowing of the alphabet by the Aramaeans can be dated between the twelfth century B. C. when they settled in the Syrian cities and came into contact with Phoenician civilization, and the end of the tenth century, the date of the earliest Aramaic inscriptions in the Phoenician

[46] This is regular in Assyrian; cf. F. W. Geers, "The Treatment of Emphatics in Akkadian," *JNES* IV (1945), pp. 65-67.

[47] The Aramaeans also had to adapt a twenty-two sign alphabet to their own speech which included a number of additional phonemes. They represented certain interdental spirants and emphatics not used in Phoenician by the signs for the corresponding dental and emphatic sibilants. See the references in the Appendix.

alphabet. Moreover, the close similarity of the two scripts in the ninth century shows that the borrowing took place late in our period rather than early.[48]

These facts necessitate a new view of the origin and development of the use of final *matres lectionis*. To regard their development as the spontaneous outgrowth of historical spelling must be discarded at least in part. There is small chance that historical spelling had so completely encrusted Aramaic writing in the short period between the borrowing of the alphabet and our earliest Aramaic inscriptions, as to give rise to a fully developed system of *matres lectionis*. This would involve not only a complete rejection of the phonetic principle which dominated Phoenician writing but a very rapid breakdown in Aramaic phonology, about which we otherwise know nothing.[49]

It is simpler to assume that an occasional historical spelling (e. g., the dropping of the final *ă̄* of the first person pronominal suffix, *-iyā̆* > *î*) suggested the principle of final vowel representation. Because of its immediate practicability in the use of the script, the principle then was applied to all final vowels, and a complete scheme of final *matres lectionis* resulted.[50] We need not look for the origin of each vowel letter, therefore, in the process of historical spelling. Rather, once the idea of vowel representation was grasped, semi-vowels, and weak consonants which were homogeneous with certain vowels were readily pressed into service: *yodh* for final *ī*, *waw* for final *ū* (one or both may have been suggested by historical spelling), *he* for final *ā* (perhaps suggested by consonantal *he* following *a* in the feminine singular suffix, or some similar form), and for final *ē* (perhaps suggested by the masculine singular suffix, or some similar form).

At no time is it necessary to suppose the consistent operation of historical spelling. Once the system of final vowel representation was established, the phonetic principle continued active in Aramaic orthography. When phonetic changes took place, the orthography was quickly

[48] Albright dates the borrowing of the alphabet around the tenth century, cf. *BASOR* # 90 (1943), p. 32. There are marked differences between the two scripts by the 8th century.

[49] The supposed principle of historical spelling did not persist in Aramaic, because there were frequent changes in the orthography to correspond to changes in pronunciation.

[50] F. R. Blake, "The Development of Symbols for the Vowels in the Alphabets Derived from the Phoenician," *JAOS* 60 (1940), p. 397, suggests that "a complete system of such signs indicating long vowels in all positions and its consistent use may have originated at a specific time in a single alphabet, and been copied by other forms of writing that stood in some special connection with the inventing script." With important modifications, the evidence supports this view.

adjusted, as is indicated by the considerable differences in orthography between the Old Aramaic inscriptions and those of later periods.

The use of internal *matres lectionis*, by the same token, does not seem to have arisen from the historical spelling of contracted diphthongs, but as an extension of the principles of vowel representation in the final position to the medial position. Thus the first internal *matres lectionis* which appear in the inscriptions do not represent contracted diphthongs, but rather the same vowels which they indicate in the final position (thus *waw* for *ū* in *'šwr*, No. 76).[51] It is true however, that internal *matres lectionis* are not widely used in Aramaic or Judahite until the general contraction of diphthongs took place. The consonantal signs representing these diphthongs were preserved by historical spelling, and thus became vowel letters, i. e., *yodh* for *ê*, and *waw* for *ô*. It is only in the later periods that historical spelling plays an important role in orthographic practice.

A word perhaps is necessary on the use of *aleph* as a *mater lectionis* in Aramaic. It already has been noted that in Old Aramaic, *aleph* regularly is consonantal, and is not used as a *mater lectionis*, exactly as in early Moabite and Hebrew.[52] In the final position, it is used only to indicate the emphatic state,[53] and in words where it is a root consonant. Not until later was it used as a *mater lectionis*.[54] This could only occur

[51] See the discussion of this matter in the Appendix.

[52] See the discussion in the sections on Moabite and Hebrew orthography.

[53] Contrary to the general view (cf. Bauer and Leander, *Grammatik des Biblisch-Aramäischen*, § 22), the *aleph* representing the emphatic state must be regarded as consonantal. If the form had been derived from *a-ha* > *ā*, the final *ā* would have been represented in the orthography by *he*, which is the regular sign for this vowel in all early Aramaic inscriptions, as well as Hebrew and Moabite. The origin of the article in Aramaic is to be looked for in a form like the demonstrative particle **ha'*. Cf. J. Barth, *Die Pronominalbildung in den semitischen Sprachen*, Leipzig, 1913, pp. 75 f., 133 f., for a different explanation. Rosenthal also believes the aleph was originally consonantal, *Die aramaistische Forschung*, p. 22.

[54] H. L. Ginsberg makes a case for the occurrence of *aleph* as a *mater lectionis* in the Panammu Inscriptions, "Aramaic Studies Today," pp. 233 ff. He points out a number of instances of the writing with final *aleph* of particles which commonly are proclitic (e. g., *p'* "and," Panammu I: 33?, 17; Panammu II: 22; and *w'* "and," Panammu II: 5, 6, 12), and in the word *lyl'* (which he reads **laylē*, following Ronzevalle, but this can hardly be correct). These exceptional occurrences, however, appear only in the Panammu Inscriptions, and even if correctly interpreted, are a local development which did not enter the main stream of early Aramaic orthography. This use of *aleph* does not occur in any other Aramaic inscriptions of the period, either before or after the Panammu Inscriptions. It is possible that the proclitics occasionally were felt to be separate morphological elements and *aleph* used therefore to represent final *ă*, while *he* was

after *aleph* in the final position had quiesced, especially after final *a* (as in *lamedh aleph* verbs, and the emphatic state), *aʼ* > *ā*. It then was regarded as the sign for *ā* and extended to other cases, ultimately displacing *he* as a *mater lectionis.*

reserved for final *ā*. It is not difficult to imagine that frequent use of *ā* followed by consonantal *aleph* might give rise to such a practice. Whether or not Ginsberg may be followed to this extent, however, is problematical, and must await better interpretation of the Panammu Inscriptions. In any event, this use of *aleph* is limited entirely to the peculiar Panammu Inscriptions, and does not influence the evolution of early standard Old Aramaic orthography.

Chapter III

EARLY MOABITE ORTHOGRAPHY

The Meša' Stone (ca. 835 b. c) is the only extant source for the language and orthographic practice of ancient Moab. The text has been treated by most of the competent Semitists of the past eighty years.[1] While the details of translation have largely been clarified, the morphological peculiarities of the language have never adequately been described. For this reason the problem of orthographic analysis remains exceedingly difficult. The chief points at issue are (1) the status of the diphthongs *aw* and *ay*, (2) the vocalization of the third person masculine singular suffix.

The evidence of the inscription is not uniform with regard to the contraction of diphthongs. Normally, the diphthongs are not indicated in the orthography, and the natural conclusion is that they have been contracted. On the other hand, there are a few cases in which the diphthong is represented in the orthography. This stands in marked contrast to the Phoenician inscriptions, in which contraction of diphthongs is regular, and the Aramaic inscriptions in which there is no contraction.

The 3rd m. s. suffix is written simply with *he* in this inscription. The problem is whether it is to be vocalized *ô* as in Hebrew, or *eh* as in Aramaic. The writers' preference is for the latter, though perhaps a combination of readings is required.[2]

[1] The standard edition of the Meša' Inscription was prepared by R. Smend and A. Socin, *Die Inschrift des Königs Mesa von Moab*, Text und Tafel, Freiburg, 1886. The most important of the early studies was that of Nöldeke, *Die Inschrift des Königs Mesa von Moab*, Kiel, 1870. A complete bibliography to 1898 will be found in Lidzbarski's *Handbuch der nordsemitischen Epigraphik*, pp. 39 ff., for transcription and facsimile, *Text*, pp. 415-416, *Atlas*, Plate I; cf. also his *Ephemeris für semitische Epigraphik*, I (1900-1902), pp. 1-10. Standard treatments are also to be found in Cooke, *A Text-Book of North-Semitic Inscriptions*, pp. 1-14; S. R. Driver, *Notes on the Hebrew Text and the Topography of the Books of Samuel*, pp. lxxxiv-xciv; R. Dussaud, *Les monuments palestiniens et judaïques*, Paris, 1912, pp. 4-21.

[2] The 3rd m. s. suffix appears simply as *-h* after both singular and plural nouns. By contrast, the suffix in Byblian Phoenician is written *-h* after singular nouns, but *-w* after plural nouns. In Aramaic we find *-h* and *-wh* (or *-h* and *-yh* in the Panammu Inscriptions); and in Hebrew *-h* (later *w* = *ô*), *hū*, and after plural nouns *-w* (later *-yw*), occasionally *êhū*. It will be noted that the Moabite forms correspond most closely to the Aramaic, in orthography at least. The verbal suffix in the Meša' Inscription also appears simply as *-h*.

The Meša' Inscription:

1. *'nk* (1, etc.), "I." The form may be vocalized **'anōkī* = Heb. *'ānōkî*, i. e., a rare example of defective consonantal orthography following the Phoenician pattern, probably derived from older Moabite inscriptions.[3] On the other hand, the form may be read **'anōk*, the final *-i* having been dropped in Moabite. It need scarcely be mentioned that long and short forms of the pronouns and pronominal suffixes occur side by side in the various Northwest Semitic dialects.[4]

2. *mš'* (1), "*Meša'*," Heb. *mêša'*, LXX Μωσα. If the stem is *yš'*, the form may be derived from either **mawša'* or **mayša'*, more likely the latter. Other derivations are also possible, however.

3. *m'b* (1, etc.), "Moab." Read **mô'āb* < **maw'ab*; the original diphthong has contracted and is not indicated in the orthography.[5]

4. *hdybny* (1/2), "the Daibonite," **had-daybōnî*.[6] The diphthong is preserved, cp. *dybn* (21). The Massoretic Text reads *dîbōn*, but the diphthong is still preserved correctly in the LXX, Δαιβων (or contracted, Δηβων in Isa. 15:2).

5. *'by* (2, etc.), "my father," **'abî*.

6. *št* (2, etc.), "years" (literally, "year"). This form agrees with North Israelite and Phoenician against Judahite *šnh*. Vocalize **šat* < **šant*.

7. *mlkty* (2/3), "I reigned," **malaktî*.

8. *w'š* (3), "and I made." This is the so-called apocopated imperfect following *waw* conversive: **wa'á'aś* < **wa'a'śē* < **wa'a'śiy* < **wa'a'śiyu*.

9. *bqrḥh* (3), "in *Qrḥh*." The vocalization is uncertain; perhaps read **qᵉriḥō*, on the pattern of *yᵉrīḥō* in the Massoretic Text.

10. *ky* (4, etc.), "for," **kī*.

[3] Compare the two forms *'nk* and *'nky* in the Panammu Inscriptions (Pan. I: 1, and Pan. II: 19). For standard Canaanite usage, see the Kilamuwa Inscription, *'nk* (1), Ch. I, No. 22, pronounced *'anōkī*.

[4] See the discussion of these pronominal forms in Hebrew in Chapter IV.

[5] So Albright, "The Oracles of Balaam," *JBL* 63 (1944), p. 211, n. 14.

[6] The writers suggest that the original form of the demonstrative in Northwest Semitic, from which the article in Hebrew and Aramaic was derived, was **ha'*. Attached proclitically in Hebrew, the *aleph* quiesced or was assimilated to the following consonant. Attached enclitically in Aramaic, the *he* was elided in the singular (**-ha'* > **-a'*, and ultimately > *-ā*), and assimilated in the plural (**-ayha'* > **ayya'* > *-ayyā*), cf. Bauer and Leander, *Grammatik des Biblisch-Aramäischen*, § 22. For a general treatment of the article in Hebrew and Aramaic, see J. Barth, *Sprachwissenschaftliche Untersuchungen zum Semitischen*, Leipzig, 1907, pp. 47-58.

11. *hš'ny* (4), "he saved me" = Heb. *hôšî'anî*. The orthography indicates that the diphthong has been contracted (*aw* > *ô*).

12. *hr'ny* (4), literally, "he caused me to see" = Heb. *hir'anî*.

13. *šn'y* (4), "my enemies" = Heb. *šōn*^{e}*'ay*.

14. *'mry* (4/5, etc.), "Omri" = Heb. *'omrî*.

15. *wy'nw* (5), "and he oppressed." Read probably **waya'anniw* or the like. Unlike the parallel form in Hebrew, the weak third radical (*waw*) is preserved.

16. *b'rṣh* (5/6), "against his land." The form may tentatively be vocalized **ba'arṣeh*.[7] Cf. Nos. 17 and 27.

17. *wyḥlph* (6), "and [his son] succeeded him." The 3rd m. s. suffix after the imperfect seems to be simply *-eh* as in Aramaic. By contrast the Hebrew form is *-ehū*, written with final *waw* for *ū* (cf. *wy'lhw*, Lachish Letter IV: 6/7, *waya'lēhū*). Final vowels regularly are represented in the Meša' Inscription, and if the *ū* of the suffix had been retained, we would expect it to be indicated in the orthography.[8] If the verbal suffix, then, was *-eh*, with loss of the final vowel, it follows that the suffix with nouns was formed along the same lines, i. e., *-ihū* > *-ih* > *-eh*, as in Aramaic. The question cannot finally be decided because the vowel letter *he*, in Moabite as well as Hebrew may represent either *ô* or *ē*. Cf. No. 27.

18. *bnh* (6), "his son," **bineh*.

19. *h'* (6), "he, that one," **hū'*.

20. *''nw* (6), "I will afflict," **'a'anniw* or the like. Cf. No. 15.

21. *bymy* (6), "in my days," **bayamay*.

22. *w'r'* (7), "and I saw" = Heb. *wā'ēre'*. Cf. No. 8.

23. *bh* (7), "on him," **beh*.

24. *wbbth* (7), "and on his dynasty." Read **babêteh* or the like. The diphthong has been contracted (*ay* > *ê*) as generally in this inscription. See the discussion under No. 59, *bbyth* (25).

[7] This was Albright's view in 1925, "Further Observations on the Name *Yahweh* and Its Modifications in Proper Names," *JBL* XLIV (1925), pp. 161-162. The arguments adduced against the vocalization *ô* for the 3rd m. s. suffix in Moabite are not decisive, since we have the same representation of the suffix in pre-exilic Hebrew inscriptions (*-h*), where the vocalization certainly is *ô*. On the whole, however, the reading **-eh* seems more likely.

[8] It cannot be maintained that there was a serious attempt to duplicate the phonetic consonantism of the Phoenician inscriptions in the Meša' Stone. Contrary to Phoenician practice, *matres lectionis* are used consistently in the final position. With the possible exception of the word *'nk* (cf. No. 1), all final vowels are represented.

25. *wyrš* (7), "and [Omri] took possession" = Heb. *wayyîraš*.

26. *mhdb'* (8), "Medeba," Heb. *mêdᵉbā'*. Read perhaps **mêhadba'*. The LXX offers a number of different transliterations: Μαιδαβα, Δαιδαβαν, Μηδαβα, etc. The modern name is *Madaba.* Whatever the correct vocalization, the *he* can hardly be regarded as an internal vowel letter.[9]

27. *ymh* (8), "his days." The reading is highly probable, but not absolutely certain.[10] Read **yamêh* for older **yamayh* < **yamayhŭ*, with contraction of the diphthong of the construct plural before the suffix. Cp. *ršh*, "its chiefs (?)" (20); but note *š'ryh* (22), "its gates," in which the construct plural apparently is not contracted before the suffix (fem. sing.). The suffix here corresponds to Aramaic forms in *-*ayh* (-*yh*),[11] later Aramaic -*êh*. The final vowel of the original suffix -*hŭ* was dropped in Moabite as in Aramaic, in contrast with Canaanite. This implies for the 3rd m. s. suffix the reading -*eh* rather than -*ô* < -*ahū*; cf. Nos. 16, 18, 23, 24, etc.

28. *wḥṣy* (8), "and a part (literally: half) of," **waḥaṣī*.

29. *ymy* (8), "the days of," **yamê*. The diphthong of the construct plural apparently has contracted, cf. No. 27. The final *yodh* therefore reflects the sound *ê* < *ay*. This shows that two distinct *e* sounds were recognized in Moabite, as also in Hebrew:[12] *ē* < *ī*, which uniformly is indicated in the orthography by *he* (cf. No. 45, *yhwh*, **yahwē*; Heb. *zh*, Ch. IV, No. 21; Aram. *'nh*, Ch. II, No. 6; etc.), and *ê* < *ay*, which is represented in the orthography by *yodh*. This use of *yodh* as a *mater lectionis* for *ê* apparently arose out of the continued spelling of the diphthong with *yodh*, although diphthongs had contracted. That the contraction of diphthongs was a recent development in 9th century Moabite is clear from the sporadic occurrence of diphthongs, particularly in place-names. Thus we have in Moabite an important modification of the Old Aramaic system of spelling, under the influence of phonetic change in the language (i. e., the contraction of diphthongs). To this may be compared the similar development in Judahite after 587 B. C., when, with the general contraction of diphthongs *yodh* came into use as a *mater lectionis* for *ê* (see Ch. IV).

[9] It is possible that the name derives from the root *db'* (cp. *db'k*, Deut. 33: 25, Ugar. *db'at*, "strength") and means "stronghold" or something comparable.

[10] Cf. Lidzbarski, *Ephemeris* I, p. 5.

[11] In the Panammu Inscriptions, *passim*.

[12] There were two distinct *e* sounds in Hebrew, as reflected in the *seghol* and *ṣere* of Massoretic Hebrew. However the Massoretic Text points to a later stage in the development of these sounds, in which *he* and *yodh* are each used with both *seghol* and *ṣere*; thus ה ֵ and י ֶ occur as well as י ֵ and ה ֶ.

30. *bnh* (8), "his son," **bineh*. This reading has been much disputed, most scholars preferring "his sons." But the expression, "half of the days of his sons," is very awkward if not actually meaningless in the context; nor does that interpretation contribute substantially to the solution of the chronological problem.[13]

31. ⌈*w*⌉*y*⌈*š*⌉*bh* (8/9), "and he restored it," **wayašibah* or the like.

32. *qrytn* (10), "Kiriathaim," Heb. *qiryātáyim*. Other forms of similar type occur in this inscription: *dbltn* (30), *ḥwrnn* (31, 32).

[13] On the chronological difficulties of this passage and suggested solutions, see Cooke, *op. cit.*, pp. 9-10. All have in common the assumption that the unnamed king of Israel against whom the Moabites revolted, was Ahab. Against this the following considerations may be urged. 1. Chronological. The 40-year datum in line 8 must be regarded as accurate, within definable limits. Comparison with the 30 years for the reign of Meša''s father (line 2) shows that the period of oppression was regarded as being substantially longer, i. e., closer to 40 years than 30 or 50; though both are round numbers and not intended to be precise to the unit (as with the other numbers in the inscription, lines 16, 20, 28, 29). The biblical figures for the reigns of the Omride dynasty are, in any case, not too low (cf. Albright, "The Chronology of the Divided Monarchy of Israel," *BASOR* # 100, pp. 20-21, fnn. 15-17). If we read, in line 8, "half the days of his son," then from the beginning of the reign of Omri to the middle of Ahab's reign we have not more than 23 years; on the other hand, if we read, "half the days of his *sons*" (i. e., including Ahaziah and Joram in the calculation), the period still does not exceed 28 or 29 years. 2. Historical. It is specifically asserted in the Bible that Meša''s revolt took place after the death of Ahab (II Kings 3: 5, cf. 1: 1). This is entirely reasonable in itself (i. e., the Moabites would hardly have revolted against a powerful monarch like Ahab; the accession of the sickly king Ahaziah would offer the desired opportunity), and should only be discounted on the basis of positive evidence to the contrary. The Meša' Stone nowhere names this king, but indicates that he is the "son of Omri" and "succeeded him" to the throne of Israel. This in itself is not decisive however, since the word *bēn* has a variety of meanings, and in the Bible is used to designate grandchildren and descendants generally, as well as sons (cf. Gen. 29: 5; 31: 28, 43; Ruth 4: 17); note also that Jehu is called "son of Omri" in Assyrian inscriptions, though this does not imply descent. That the king in question is actually the last of the house of Omri is implied in line 7, where we have an allusion to the overthrow of the Omride dynasty (cf. Montgomery, *The Books of Kings, ICC*, 1951, pp. 358-359). In the inscription, then, Meša' has passed over from Omri, who conquered the land, to Joram, in whose day the Moabites regained their independence. No special mention is made of the intervening period, because no special interest attached to it; this is characteristic of the biblical historians also (e. g., the oppressions in the Book of Judges, and notoriously in the case of the sojourn in Egypt).

Combining the biblical data and the evidence of the Meša' Stone, we have the following picture. The land of Moab was conquered by Omri and laid under tribute. This situation persisted through the reign of Ahab. After his death the machinery of revolt was set into motion, though the actual commencement of

The final syllable is to be vocalized either *-*ōn* < *-*ān*, or *-*ēn* < **ayn*.[14] The former reading is perhaps preferable. In the word *ḥwrnn*, the first syllable contains an uncontracted diphthong (*aw*); it is therefore doubtful that the final syllable would contain a contracted diphthong (*ê* < *ay*).

33. *'š* (10), "the men of," **'īš*.

34. *w'ḥzh* (11), "and I took it," **wa'ōḥizah*. The omission of the stem consonant *aleph* is an instance of phonetic as against historical spelling. On the form of the suffix see No. 17. Cp. also *w'ḥzh* (20) and *w'mr* (24).

35. *ryt* (12), "satisfaction of," **riyyat* (?) for **riwyat*, from a root *rwy*.[15]

36. *'r'l dwdh* (12), "Arel its commander," following Albright. Read **'ar'el dawideh*.[16]

37. *lpny* (13), "before," **lapanê* or **lipnê*. On the vocalization see No. 29.

38. *w'šb* (13), "and I settled (literally: caused to dwell)," **wa'ôšib*. Cf. No. 11.

39. *ly* (14), "to me," **lî*.

40. *nbh* (14), "Nebo," Heb. *nᵉbō*. This reading, proposed by Nöldeke, is generally accepted today.[17] Note that the *he* is used as a *mater lectionis* for final *ō*.

41. *bllh* (15), "at night," **balêlā*. Cp. Heb. *bᵉlaylā*. The diphthong is contracted.

42. *hṣhrm* (15), "noon-day." The ending is probably adverbial *-*am*, rather than -*aym* as in Hebrew, which would contract to *-*êm* (since the dual appears in Moabite as *-*ayn* > *-*ên*). Compare such Hebrew forms as *yômām*, *ḥinnām*, *rêqām*, *etc.* Cf. No. 32, where the mixing of similar forms is discussed.

hostilities is to be dated in the reign of Joram (of Israel). Thus line 8 is to be understood: the land of Medeba was occupied from the time of Omri until the middle of the reign of his (grand)son, 40 years. The two sources give supplementary accounts of the conflict, which resulted in the independence of Moab. The final notice in the Meša' Stone (line 7) records the downfall of the house of Omri.

[14] A. Ungnad, in Gressmann's *Altorientalische Texte und Bilder zum Alten Testamente* I (Text), Tübingen, 1909, p. 172, reads -*ōn*. Nöldeke, *op. cit.*, pp. 33-34, prefers -*ên*. On the interchange of the endings -*ān*, -*ayn*, and -*ām*, -*aym*, in place names, cf. Brockelmann, *Grundriss der vergleichenden Grammatik der semitischen Sprachen*, § 216.

[15] W. F. Albright, "Two Little Understood Amarna Letters from the Middle Jordan Valley," *BASOR* # 89 (1943), p. 16, n. 55.

[16] *Ibid.*

[17] Nöldeke, *op. cit.*, p. 12.

43. *hḥrmth* (17), "I devoted it." Vocalize perhaps **haḥrimtîh* or the like. For the form compare Syriac **qṭaltîh* the *peal* perfect 2nd f. s. with 3rd f. s. suffix. See the discussion of the feminine suffix under No. 51.

44. [*k*]*ly* (17/18), "the vessels of," **kilê*, or the like, Heb. *k*ᵉ*lê*. Cf. No. 29.

45. *yhwh* (18), "Yahweh," **yahwē* < **yahwiy*(*u*). The *he* is a *mater lectionis* for final *ē*.

46. *w'sḥb . hm* (18), "and I dragged them." The suffix is separated by a word divider, and is to be regarded as an independent pronominal element, as in Aramaic. Read **him* < **himma*.

47. *bnh* (18), "he built," **banā* < **banaya*.

48. *by* (19), "against me," **bî*.

49. *m'tn* (20), "two hundred," **ma'tên* < **ma'tayn*, Heb. *m'tym*.

50. *ršh* (20), "its chiefs (?)." If the interpretation is correct, the form is equivalent to Hebrew *r'šyw*. On the suffix cf. No. 27.

51. *š'ryh* (22), "its gates." Read perhaps **ša'arayh* (without contraction of the diphthong), following the pattern of the plural noun with pronominal suffix in Old Aramaic. On the other hand **ša'arê-h* (with contraction of the diphthong) is also possible. In that case the *yodh* would be regarded as a final *mater lectionis*, and the pronominal suffix as a separate element (as often in the Panammu Inscriptions).

52. *bnty* (22), "I built," = Heb. *bānîtî*.

53. *mgdlth* (22), "its towers." Vocalize **magdalōtêh* or the like, < **magdalōtayh*(*a*). From the orthography it is clear that the diphthong has been contracted. See the discussion under No. 59.

54. *bt mlk* (23), "the palace," = Heb. *bêt mélek*.

55. *kl'y* (23), "the retaining walls of" or "the pair of." The form is construct plural or dual in *ê*. Cf. No. 29.

56. [*lm'*]*yn* ?(23), "for the spring," **lamma'yān*. The stone actually has only *'šw* [ ]*yn*. But the commonly proposed *lmyn*, "for water," is unacceptable, both because of the context, and because the uncontracted form of the word on the basis of the evidence is improbable (we would expect **mên* < **mayn*). The situation presented in the inscription is that the king has determined to insure an adequate water supply for the city, and goes about this by, (1) constructing dam walls to conserve the flow of water from the spring or digging out the spring and building up the walls of the pool so formed, to serve as a reservoir, and (2) ordering the people to dig cisterns in their courtyards. The emendation [*lm'*]*yn* labors under one difficulty, namely the restricted

size of the lacuna. Lidzbarski believes that there is room only for three letters (*'św[ḥ lm]yn*) on the basis of his measurements.[18] But *ayin* is a small letter in the Meša' Inscription, and fits over the understroke of the *yodh* so as to occupy very little additional space (note the sequence *ayin yodh* at the end of line 27).

57. *'n* (24), "there was not," **'ên* < **'ayn*, Heb. *'áyin*.

58. *'św* (24), "make (imperative)," *'aśū* < **'asiyū*. Cf. No. 8.

59. *bbyth* (25), "in his house," **babayteh* or **babêteh*. Compare *bbth* (7), No. 24. This orthographic confusion in Moabite illustrates an uncertainty in the treatment of diphthongs which is unparalleled in early Northwest Semitic inscriptions. The presence of the two forms listed above in the same inscription can be explained only in one of the following ways: (1) historical spelling; the diphthong has been contracted, but the *yodh* representing it is preserved in certain cases in the orthography; (2) language in the process of phonetic change; the diphthongs are in the process of contraction, and there is confusion as to which is the correct form, or either form may be regarded as correct; (3) dialectal mixture; to a certain extent the contracted forms and uncontracted forms may be classified, and the differences may be due to differences in the speech of the Moabites; (4) error.

Because historical spelling can only have been of very recent origin in Moabite at this period,[19] alternatives one and two actually fall together. This has been discussed at some length under No. 29, and seems the most probable explanation of the phenomena. There is reason to believe, however, that alternative three may offer help in the clarification of the linguistic picture in Moab. It is possible that in the speech of the royal court, and of the educated and commercial classes, diphthongs were contracted,[20] while in the speech of the rural classes, the older traditional pronunciation, with diphthongs uncontracted, was preserved. In any case, the fluid treatment of diphthongs in the inscription shows that the

[18] *Ephemeris* I, pp. 7-8.

[19] The introduction of *matres lectionis* in Moabite writing cannot be much earlier than 900 B.C. There is evidence to show that Hebrew was still being written defectively in the 10th century, while a system of *matres lectionis* was adopted apparently in the 9th century. The development of *matres lectionis* in Aramaic seems to have taken place toward the end of the 10th century (cf. Ch. II).

[20] Perhaps the court speech was modelled after or influenced by North Israelite speech. From the time of the conquest by David, Moab was tied to the United Monarchy and then to the Northern Kingdom with minor breaks until the time of Meša'. Since diphthongs regularly were contracted in the speech of the Northern Kingdom, this may have influenced the speech of the upper classes and court circles in Moab.

scribe is free to choose between two pronunciations. The majority of forms (including idiomatic expressions) show contraction, and this may reflect the sophisticated speech of the capital; on the other hand, place names preserve uncontracted diphthongs and this may reflect the native speech of ordinary Moabites.

60. *ʿyn* (27), "ruins," Hebrew *ʿiyyīn*!

61. *bt dbltn* (30), "Beth Diblathaim"; for the vocalization, see No. 32.

62. *ḥwrnn* (31, 32), "Horonaim," **ḥawrōnān* or **ḥawrōnên*. Cf. No. 32.

As in Aramaic, final vowels in Moabite are represented consistently by *matres lectionis.*

The final vowel *ī* is represented by *yodh*: Nos. 4, 5, 7, 10, 11, 12, 14, 28, 39, 48 and 52.

The final vowel *ū* is represented by *waw*: No. 58.

The final vowel *ā* is represented by *he*: Nos. 41 and 47.

The final vowel *ē* is represented by *he*: No. 45.

The final vowel *ō* is represented by *he*: Nos. 9 (?) and 40.

The diphthong *ay* is represented by the consonantal element, *yodh*: Nos. 4, 13, 21, 51?, and 59?. Of these, the diphthongs in Nos. 13 and 21 resulted from the doubling of the semi-vocalic element.

The diphthong *aw* is represented by *waw*: No. 62.

The contracted diphthong *ê* (< *ay*) in the final position is represented by *yodh*: Nos. 29, 37, 44 and 55.

There are a number of cases of the contraction of diphthongs in the medial position (zero in the orthography):

ay > *ê*, Nos. 2?, 24, 27, 41, 49, 50?, 53, 54, 57 and 61.

aw > *ô*, Nos. 3, 11 and 38.

There is no evidence for the use of internal *matres lectionis.*

The use of *matres lectionis* in the Mešaʿ Stone is essentially the same as in the Old Aramaic inscriptions.[21] The only variations requiring comment are the use of *yodh* to represent the contracted diphthong (*ay* > *ê*) in the final position (see No. 29), and the extension in the use of *he* to signify final *ō*.[22] As will be shown, the same system also was used in

[21] For details, see Ch. II. Internal *matres lectionis* do not appear in Aramaic inscriptions until the late 8th century. The orthographic peculiarities of the Panammu Inscriptions are a special development and do not represent standard Aramaic orthography; see the discussion in the Appendix. *Aleph* does not appear as a *mater lectionis* in standard Old Aramaic, Moabite or Hebrew inscriptions.

[22] It is quite possible that *he* also represented *ô* in Aramaic, but the usage has not turned up in the inscriptional material thus far. The chief reason is that

Hebrew after the 10th century B. C. It is scarcely probable that the same scheme of *matres lectionis* developed independently in the orthography of each of three neighboring countries. It appears rather that the use of *matres lectionis* began among Aramaic speaking people (in the 10th century?) and then spread rapidly to all other peoples using the Phoenician alphabet, except the Phoenicians themselves whose traditions prevented a major change in orthographic practice. This was the period of greatest Aramaean expansion, during which they became dominant politically in Syria, and developed extensive commercial relations with the nations to the West and South as well as to the East. Along with commercial products, they seem to have exported unwittingly a new system of improved spelling, a system which had sufficient practicability to be adopted, almost immediately, by the Moabites and Israelites.[23]

there are very few cases of final ô in Aramaic, and the form would be limited to proper names, place names and the like. The use of *he* for final ô is found also in the Hebrew inscriptions of the 8th century and following. Such an extension in usage is readily explicable in Hebrew and Moabite. In *lamedh yodh* verbs, *he* is used regularly as a *mater lectionis* for final ā and ē, in different forms; it would be most natural to use the same sign to represent the infinitive absolute of these verbs in ō.

[23] *A priori*, it is possible that the system of vowel letters originated in Moab or Israel, and spread over the Aramaean world; but this is much less likely. In the late 10th century, Israelite orthography still followed Phoenician principles of defective writing. Almost contemporary Aramaic inscriptional material already employed *matres lectionis* in the final position.

Furthermore, Phoenician influence on Israel, and to a lesser extent on Moab, was always greater than on Aram. In matters of language, particularly orthography, the difference would be decisive. Moabite and Israelite, being Canaanite dialects, would lend themselves readily to Phoenician spelling rules. Aramaic, on the other hand, differed considerably from the Phoenician of this period; immediate adaptation of the alphabet was necessary, and other changes would follow in short order. It can hardly be doubted that 1) the complete system of *matres lectionis* in the final position was created at a single time, and 2) the center of radiation was Syria, among the Aramaeans.

Chapter IV

EARLY HEBREW ORTHOGRAPHY

Two phases in the evolution of early Hebrew orthography may be distinguished. The older phase, extending down to the 10th century B. C., is represented by the Gezer Calendar (ca. 925 B. C.).[1] The later phase covers the period from the 9th century to the fall of Judah (587 B. C.). The analysis will include only those inscriptions which contain sufficient decipherable material to be of orthographic interest: the Shemaiah Seal from the 9th century,[2] the Beth Horon Sherd (early 8th century),[3] the Samaria Ostraca (ca. 778-770 B. C.),[4] the Siloam Inscription (ca. 700 B. C.),[5] the Ophel Ostracon and the Silwan Inscription (7th century

[1] The literature on the Gezer Calendar is very extensive. A bibliography of the early treatments of this text is to be found in Diringer's *Le iscrizioni antico-ebraiche palestinesi,* Florence, 1934, pp. 18-20; his discussion is on pp. 1-18, Plates I and II. The most important recent treatment is that of W. F. Albright, "The Gezer Calendar," *BASOR* # 92 (1943), pp. 16-26; an extensive bibliography is to be found in the notes to this article. Additional material may be found in U. Cassuto, *Studi e Materiali di Storia della Religioni* XII (1936), pp. 107-125 (not available); S. Birnbaum, "The Dates of the Gezer Tablet and of the Samaria Ostraca," *PEQ* 1942, pp. 104-108, and "On the Possibility of Dating Hebrew Inscriptions," *PEQ* 1944, pp. 213-217. D. Diringer, "The Dating of Early Hebrew Inscriptions (The Gezer Tablet and the Samaria Ostraca)," *PEQ* 1943, pp. 50-54, and "Note on the Dating of Early Hebrew Inscriptions," *PEQ* 1945, pp. 53-54. G. R. Driver, "Brief Notes," *PEQ* 1945, pp. 5-9. E. Zolli, "La tavoletta di Gezer," *Biblica* 27 (1946), pp. 129-131. H. Torczyner, "להבנתו של לוח גזר" (English Title: "A New Interpretation of the Gezer Calendar"), *BJPES* XIII (1946-47), pp. 1-7. J. G. Février, "Remarques sur le Calendrier de Gezer," *Semitica* I (1948), pp. 33-41.

[2] This seal is discussed in Diringer, *Le iscrizioni antico-ebraiche palestinesi,* pp. 199-200, Plate XX, No. 10. He also gives an extensive bibliography. The seal is important principally because of its early date. For later periods inscriptional material is available.

[3] B. Maisler, "Excavations at Tell Qasile," *BJPES* XV: 1-2 (NS 1949), pp. 8-18, Pl. V, 1.

[4] The standard edition of the Samaria Ostraca is Reisner, Fisher and Lyon, *Harvard Excavations at Samaria,* I (Text), Cambridge, 1924, pp. 227-246. For discussion and bibliography, see Diringer, *Le iscrizioni antico-ebraiche palestinesi,* pp. 21-74. The Gezer Calendar and the Samaria Ostraca were written in the North Israelite dialect, in which diphthongs regularly were contracted, in contrast with the Southern Judahite dialect, in which they were not. The other inscriptions treated are in the Southern dialect. On the date of the Ostraca, cf. Albright, "A Reëxamination of the Lachish Letters," *BASOR* # 73 (1939), p. 21, n. 38, and *Archaeology and the Religion of Israel,* pp. 41, 214, n. 41.

[5] For discussion and bibliography, see Diringer, *Le iscrizioni antico-ebraiche palestinesi,* pp. 81-102.

B. C.),[6] the Stamped Jar Handles (7th and early 6th centuries),[7] and the Lachish Letters (ca. 589 B. C.).[8]

The Gezer Calendar:

1. *yrḥw* (1 bis, etc.), "his two months," **yarḥêw*, following Albright. This form has provoked considerable discussion among scholars, and a wide variety of explanations have been offered. All earlier suggestions must be discarded because of the failure to observe epigraphic, orthographic or hermeneutic requirements. The best of these was made by Ginsberg, who described the form as an old nominative dual construct, **yarḥā* > **yarḥō*. The *waw* was taken to be a vowel letter representing final *ō*.[9] This, however, involves an orthographic anachronism, since final *ō* is always represented by *he* and never by *waw* in pre-exilic Hebrew inscriptions.[10] Albright's solution alone meets the necessities of the case.[11]

[6] For the Ophel Ostracon, see Diringer, *Le iscrizioni antico-ebraiche palestinesi*, pp. 74-79. Albright fixes the date in the 7th century, "Notes on Early Hebrew and Aramaic Epigraphy," *JPOS* 6 (1926), pp. 88-93. Cf. also Torczyner, "כתובות השלוח לוח גזר וחרס העופל," *BJPES* VII (1939), pp. 6 ff. E. L. Sukenik, "על חרס העופל," *BJPES* XIII (1946-47), pp. 115-118.

On the Silwan Inscription, see Diringer, *op. cit.*, pp. 105-110, for discussion and bibliography.

[7] These are dated by Ginsberg from about 666 B. C. to 587 B. C., "MMŠT and MṢH," *BASOR* # 109 (1948), p. 20. See also Diringer, *op. cit.*, pp. 145-157, Plate XVIII.

[8] The standard edition of the Lachish Letters is H. Torczyner (*et al.*), *Lachish I: The Lachish Letters*, London, 1938. For bibliography, see the following articles: W. F. Albright, "A Supplement to Jeremiah: The Lachish Ostraca," *BASOR* # 61 (1936), pp. 10-16; "The Oldest Hebrew Letters: The Lachish Ostraca," *BASOR* # 70 (1938), pp. 11-17; "A Reëxamination of the Lachish Letters," *BASOR* # 73 (1939), pp. 16-21; "The Lachish Letters after Five Years," *BASOR* # 82 (1941), pp. 18-24. H. L. Ginsberg, "Lachish Ostraca New and Old," *BASOR* # 80 (1940), pp. 10-13. More recently there has appeared H. G. May's "Lachish Letter IV: 7-10," *BASOR* # 97 (1945), pp. 22-25; and Albright's "Postscript to Professor May's article," *BASOR* # 97 (1945), p. 26.

[9] H. L. Ginsberg, *BJPES* II (1935), p. 49. This reading also is adopted by G. R. Driver, "Brief Notes," *PEQ* 1945, pp. 5 ff.

[10] For other objections to this reading, see Albright, "The Gezer Calendar," p. 24.

[11] From the orthographic point of view, the final *waw* must be either a vowel or a consonant (in this case a diphthong). If it is a vowel letter, it must represent *ū*; such a form cannot be interpreted as a nominative construct dual, which is required by the context. Besides the defective writing of *pšt* (No. 3) implies that final vowels were not indicated in the orthography of this inscription (and this agrees very well with the evidence of the contemporary Phoenician inscriptions). If the *waw* is consonantal, then it must indicate the 3rd m. s. suffix. On Albright's interpretation of the phrase, "his two months," cf. "The Gezer

The vocalization of the suffix, **-êw*[12] < *êhū* < **-ayhū*, follows North Israelite pronunciation, in which the contraction of the diphthong, *ay* > *ê*, preceded the syncope of intervocalic *he*.[13] The yodh of the suffix in the Kethib of the Massoretic text (*-yw*) is reminiscent of the pronunciation **-êw*. Only in a dialect in which the diphthong *ay* was preserved, would a form *-aw* < **-ayhū* result.[14]

2. *yrḥ* (3, 4, etc.), "his month," **yarḥô*.[15] The parallelism requires the suffix here; cf. No. 1. The absence of a *mater lectionis* to indicate final *ô*,[16] shows that in the 10th century, Hebrew orthography followed the Phoenician principle of phonetic consonantism.[17]

3. *pšt* (3), "flax," *pištā*, following Yeivin and Albright.[18] The word is written defectively, without orthographic indication of the final vowel.

4. *qṣ* (7), "summer-fruit," *qêṣ*, Biblical Hebrew, *qáyiṣ*. The contraction of the diphthong *ay* > *ê*, indicates that the dialect of the Gezer Calendar was North Israelite, as opposed to Judahite.

The Shemaiah Seal:

This is the only seal extant which can be dated to the 9th century with any confidence.[19] The dating depends largely upon the presence of

Calendar," p. 22, n. 28. Another possibility has been suggested to the writers by Dr. P. Skehan of Catholic University: this may be an idiomatic expression, involving a prospective suffix, in apposition with the following noun, i. e., "two months of it, of . . . . ." On the occurrence of this construction in the Old Testament, cf. *G–K*, § 128d, 131r. It also has turned up in the new Karatepe Inscriptions, and may now be identified in other Phoenician inscriptions. This is the ביתו משה construction discussed by Gordon in "Azitawadd's Phoenician Inscription," *JNES* VIII (1949), pp. 113-114: *lšbtnm dnnym* B: I: 17 and *ltty b'l*, B: III: 4; cp. also *Eshmun'azar*, line 1, *lmlky mlk*, etc.

[12] On this form cf. Albright, "The Gezer Calendar," p. 22 n. 27.

[13] The evidence of the Phoenician texts, Amarna and Egyptian transliterations, indicates that this contraction was general at a very early period. Cf. Harris, *Development of the Canaanite Dialects*, pp. 29 ff.

[14] For the form **-aw*, see the discussion under No. 68, *'nšw*. The contraction **-ayhū* > *-aw*, took place in Aramaic, with the further development, **-awhi* > *-ôhī*. This would be expected in North Israelite as well, if the suffix were **-aw*.

[15] Albright, "The Gezer Calendar," pp. 22, 24.

[16] In later inscriptions, the suffix *-ô* is indicated by the vowel letter *he*; cf. No. 23 (Siloam), and regularly in the Lachish Letters. On the vocalization of *r'w* (Siloam) see the discussion under No. 26.

[17] In all probability under direct Phoenician influence which was at its height in Israel during the 10th century. See Albright, "The Phoenician Inscriptions of the Tenth Century B. C. from Byblus," pp. 159-160.

[18] S. Yeivin, *The History of the Jewish Script* (in Hebrew), I, Jerusalem, 1939, p. 159; Albright, "The Gezer Calendar," p. 22, n. 34; "The Oracles of Balaam," p. 211, n. 12.

[19] Following Albright (personal communication).

a single extremely archaic *mem*, for which parallels can be found only in the Gezer Calendar and the Byblian Inscriptions of the 10th century. Other characters, however, closely resemble early 8th century forms (particularly the *waw*). The logical date, therefore, is sometime in the 9th century B. C.

5. *lšmʿyhw,* "belonging to Shemaiah," Biblical Hebrew, *šᵉmaʿyāhū*. The final vowel *ū* is represented by the vowel letter *waw*. If the dating of the seal is correct, this is the first instance of a *mater lectionis* in Hebrew orthography.[20] Note also the name *ʿzryhw* (Biblical Hebrew *ʿᵃzaryāhū*) on the same seal.

The Beth Horon Sherd:

6. *byt,* "the temple [of Horon]." The orthography is anomalous, since the diphthong in this word is left uncontracted (as in Judahite), while in the word immediately following (No. 7), the diphthong is contracted (*ḥôrōn* < **ḥawrān*), as in North Israelite. One may compare with this the place name *ḥwrnn* in the Mešaʿ Stone, Ch. III, No. 62 (oddly enough, most diphthongs in this inscription are contracted). Most apparent inconsistencies in orthographic practice occur in proper names or place names; this suggests that they are to be accounted for by dialectal mixture in pronunciation.[20a]

7. *ḥrn,* "[the god] Horon," see No. 6.

The Samaria Ostraca:

8. *lšmryw* (# 1, etc.),[21] "to Shemariah," **šᵉmaryaw*. The theophorous element, **yaw* < *yahū*, is not further contracted, since the syncope of intervocalic *he* was of recent origin, and took place after the period of general contraction of diphthongs in Canaanite.[22] Proper names with this ending, *-yw*, are common in the Samaria Ostraca.

[20] The fact that a full system of *matres lectionis* was employed in the Mešaʿ Inscription from the middle of the 9th century, suggests strongly that they were being used in Israel at the same time.

[20a] Not a few of these inconsistencies involve specifically the exchange of the forms *bt/byt*, both in place names and in other usages (cf. Chap. III, No. 59), which suggests the possibility that we are dealing actually with metaplastic forms which existed side by side. For a similar problem, *confer* the several isolated forms in ancient South Arabic (*e. g., ym, ywm,* etc.; see below, No. 49) which are exchanged regularly in the inscriptions. Yet there can be no question of a general contraction of diphthongs in South Arabic, and the script is rigidly consonantal.

[21] The numbers in parentheses represent the different ostraca, following the enumeration of the official edition.

[22] Later (after the Exile?), the element **yaw* prefixed to proper names was contracted to **yô-* (Massoretic יְהוֹ), along with the general contraction of diphthongs (*aw* and *ay*) in this period.

9. *b'rym* (# 1), "Beer-yam (?)," **bi'r-yam*. The reading **bi'raym* is equally possible, but that would reflect the Judahite pronunciation of the place name. Presumably the diphthong would be contracted in Israelite pronunciation. The location of the place is not known.

10. *'z'* (# 1), "Uzza," **'uzza'*. The *aleph* is a hypocoristic ending, probably still consonantal. Compare the name *'bd'* in the Byblian inscriptions,[23] and also in Ostracon # 57; cp. *b'l'* (# 1), etc.

11. *'zh* (# 2, 17), a place name. The *he* probably is a *mater lectionis*; the vocalization of the word may be **'azā* or **'azō*, or something similar.

12. *qṣh* (# 4, 5, etc.), "Qoṣe (?)." The vocalization is uncertain. The *he* apparently is a vowel letter.

13. *yn* (# 11, 12, etc.), "wine," **yên* < **yayn*.

14. *'ḥzy* (# 25), "Aḥzay," Biblical Hebrew *'aḥzay*. The diphthong regularly was preserved in hypocoristic endings of this kind.

15. *b'lm'ny* (# 27), "Baalmeonite," **ba'l-me'ōnî*. The *yodh* is a *mater lectionis* for final *î*.

16. *'lh* (# 38), a proper name. The *he* apparently is a *mater lectionis*, but the vocalization is unknown.[24]

17. *ḥglh* (# 47, cf. # 45), "Hoglah," **ḥoglā*; Biblical Hebrew, *bêt ḥoglā*, etc.

18. *n'h* (# 50), "Neah," **ne'ā* = Biblical *nē'ā* (?), cf. *nō'ā*, Num. 26 : 33, etc.

19. *yḥw'ly* (# 55, 60), "Yeḥaweli," **yeḥaw'elî*. Cp. Biblical *'ly*, Egyptian Aramaic *yhw'ly* (?), Ugar. *'ly*, and Phoen. *yḥwmlk*.[25] The first element is a *piel* jussive of **ḥwy*, in which the diphthong normally is preserved, *-aw* < **-awwiy(u)*.

The Siloam Inscription:

20. ⌜*h*⌝*nqbh* (1). This probably is the same word as No. 23, but the context is not clear in this instance.

21. *wzh* (1), "and this" = Biblical *wezē*.

22. *hyh* (1, 6), "was" = Biblical *hāyā*.

23. *hnqbh* (1, 4), literally, "its being tunneled through," **hinnaqibô* or the like. The gender of the suffix cannot be fixed, since the word for

[23] Cf. Ch. I, No. 21.

[24] Cp. the proper name *ymnh* in the "Barley check of Samaria" (before 722 B. C.). Cf. Diringer, *Le iscrizioni antico-ebraiche palestinesi*, pp. 70 ff.; Albright, "Ostracon C 1101 of Samaria," *PEFQS* 1936, pp. 211-215.

[25] Cf. Albright, *Archaeology and the Religion of Israel*, p. 202, n. 18.

tunnel in classical Hebrew is not known, but it probably was masculine. Cp. Arabic *naqbu*^{n}, Syriac *neqbā*, Accadian *naqbu*, Neo-Hebrew *néqeb*, Proto-Sinaitic *nqbn* (Albright); on the other hand, late Hebrew has *nqwbh*, Biblical *maqqébet*, "hole," etc. This form must be taken together with *lhnqb* (2) and *hnqbh* in the phrase *wbym hnqbh*, "when it was tunneled through," and construed as a verbal noun of some kind. To read the *niphal* infinitive is particularly suitable. Cf. No. 20.[26]

24. *bʿwd* (2), "while yet," **baʿawd*. The diphthong is uncontracted in Judahite.

25. *ʾš* (2 bis, 4), "one, each," *ʾīš*.

26. *rʿw* (2, 3, 4), "the other," literally, "his fellow," **reʿew*, Biblical *rēʿēhū*.[27] The form *rēʿô* in Jeremiah 6:21 is anomalous, and should be repointed **rēʿēw* < *rēʿēhū* (with syncope of the *he*).[28]

27. *ql* (2), "the voice of," **qāl*.[29] The form **qawl*, later *qôl* (Biblical Hebrew), would have been written *qwl*,[30] in this inscription.

28. *ky* (3), "for," *kī*.

29. *hyt* (3), "was," **hayat*; this is the older form of the 3rd f. s. perfect of *lamedh he* verbs. Cp. II Kings 9:37, Kethib.

30. *zdh* (3). The meaning and vocalization are uncertain. The *he* probably is a vowel letter for the *ā* of the feminine ending.[31]

31. *wbym* (3), "and on the day of," **wabayām*. Cf. No. 27. The form is discussed under No. 49, *kym* (frequent in the Lachish Letters). This form does not occur in the Massoretic text, the alternative **yawm* > *yôm* having been levelled through.

[26] This was proposed by A. Fischer, "Zur Siloahinschrift," *ZDMG* LVI (1902), pp. 800 ff. He read the feminine suffix, however.

[27] So Bergsträsser, *Hebräische Grammatik*, § 16e. The same development is found in the verbal suffix *-ēhū* > **ēw*, in the Nash Papyrus, line 16: *wyqdšyw* for Biblical *wyqdšhw* (Ex. 20:11).

[28] The form *rʿhw* occurs some 115 times in the Bible as against the single occurrence of *rʿw*. Nevertheless the appearance of the word in the Siloam Inscription shows that it was current in the common speech (and writing) of Jerusalem. This is one of the many small differences between the common tongue and the literary language of the time. Older, fuller forms are preserved (and restored) in the literary texts (i. e., the Bible), while the shorter forms, involving syncope of weak consonants and the loss of final vowels are preserved in the matter-of-fact language of the surviving contemporary texts. The Lachish Letters (on which see below), while formulaic, are also colloquial, and preserve the short forms of popular speech.

[29] Cf. Ch. II, No. 4.

[30] Both forms occur in Arabic.

[31] Cf. F. R. Blake, "The Word זדה in the Siloam Inscription," *JAOS* XXII (1901), pp. 55-60.

32. *hkw* (4), "they struck" = Biblical *hikkū*.

33. *wylkw* (4), "and [the water] went" = Biblical *wayyēlᵉkū*.

34. *hmym* (5), "the water," **ham-maym*.

35. *hmwṣ'* (5), "the source," **ham-mawṣa'*, Biblical Hebrew *ham-môṣā'*.

36. *hbrkh* (5), "the pool," Biblical *bᵉrēkā*.

37. *bm'tym* (5), literally, "for two hundred," **bama'taym*; cf. Biblical *mā'táyim*.

38. *'mh* (5, 6), "cubit," Biblical *'ammā*.

The Ophel Ostracon:

39. *'ḥyhw* (2), "Aḥiah," **'aḥīyahū*. Several other names, only partly preserved, have the same theophorous element, *yhw*. This indicates that in Judahite, by and large, the fuller form *yhw* was preserved, while in the North, the *he* had already been lost, *yw*.[32]

The Silwan Inscription:

40. *zh* (1), "this," *zē*. The next word is partially obliterated, so this reading is not certain. Cf. No. 21.

41. *hbyt* (1), "the house," **hab-bayt*. No other readings in this inscription are sufficiently clear for orthographic analysis.

The Stamped Jar Handles:

42. *zp, zyp*, "Ziph." The *yodh* may be a *mater lectionis* for medial *ī*, in which case it is the first instance in Hebrew epigraphic material. It postdates the first appearance of internal *matres lectionis* in Aramaic inscriptions by about a century.[33]

43. *śwkh*, "Socoh," **śawkō*.

44. *mṣh*, "?". Ginsberg considers this a contraction of *mṣph*, "Mizpah."[34]

The Lachish Letters:

45. *'dny* (# 2:1, etc.), "my lord," *'adōnî*.

46. *y'wš* (# 2:1, etc.), "Yaosh," **ya'ōš*. As Albright has shown, the name is hypocoristic; the form is the *qal* jussive of **'ūš*.[35] The *aleph*

[32] See however Ginsberg, "Lachish Notes," *BASOR* # 71 (1938), pp. 24-25. Some mixing of the forms would have been inevitable.

[33] The first true internal *matres lectionis* in Aramaic also appear in a place name, *'šwr*. Cf. Ch. II, No. 76.

[34] "MMŠT and MṢH," pp. 21-22.

[35] "A Supplement to Jeremiah: The Lachish Ostraca," *BASOR* # 61 (1936), p. 12.

apparently was in the process of quiescence, since in the spelling there is some confusion between the correct form of the name historically, **ya'ōš* (which would have been written *y'š*), and the current pronunciation, which must have sounded very much like **yawš* (which would have been written phonetically *ywš*). At this stage, the *aleph* represented the correct historical spelling, the *waw* the current pronunciation. The Massoretic text apparently preserves this mixed position in Jer. 27:1 *y'wšyhw* (Kethib), while a still later development after the contraction of the diphthong (**a'ō* > *aw* > *ô*), is represented in the standard vocalization, *yôšiyāhū* for **yôš-yāhū*.[36]

The *waw* cannot be taken as a *mater lectionis* for *ô* in this case. The usage here illustrates the tendency which ultimately resulted in the regular employment of internal *matres lectionis* (i. e., the consonantal sign used to indicate a diphthong, and then being preserved after the diphthong contracts, to signify the resulting long vowel). This practice could only develop after the contraction of diphthongs *aw* > *ô*, and *ay* > *ê*. This, as the Lachish Letters make abundantly clear, had not yet taken place in Judahite.[37]

47. *yhwh* (# 2:2, etc.), "Yahweh," **yahwē*.

48. *'t* (# 2:3, etc.), "now," **'at*, a colloquial form, corresponding to the longer literary word, *'attā*.[38] There can be no doubt that final accented *ā* would have been indicated in the orthography, as it is regularly after the 10th century in all Hebrew inscriptions.[39] In this case,

[36] The consonantal form of the name in the Bible is etymologically correct, and historically older. Very often, the Massoretic text preserves (at least in the consonantal text) older forms.

[37] The general development of *matres lectionis* seems to have been along these lines. In the case of *yodh* and *waw*, they first were used in the final position to represent *ī* and *ū* respectively. After a considerable period, their usage was extended to the medial position, with the same values. During the same period, the diphthongs *aw* and *ay* also were represented by *waw* and *yodh*. When these diphthongs were contracted, the *waw* and *yodh* were retained in the spelling, and thus became signs for *ô* and *ê*. (The preservation of these signs medially after the contraction of the diphthong, would only take place after the introduction of medial *matres lectionis* generally; in earlier times, the *waw* or *yodh* dropped out when the diphthong was contracted.) The next stage in the use of these *matres lectionis* was the extension of the *waw* for *ô* to the final position, where the *ô* formerly was represented by *he*. This unquestionably was a post-monarchic development, since 1) the diphthongs *ay* and *aw* were not yet contracted in Judahite, 2) there is not a single instance of *waw* = *ô* in any pre-exilic Hebrew inscription.

[38] Cf. Gordon, "Lachish Letter IV," *BASOR* # 67 (1937), p. 32, n. 9, who rejects the vocalization *'attā*, but reads *'ēt*.

[39] The same is true of Aramaic and Moabite. The fact is that any *final* vowel,

as in a number of others, the evidence indicates that long and short forms of the same word existed side by side, the long forms being displaced in the common speech, and surviving only in literary works. In the past, many scholars (including the Massoretes) have generalized a particular vocalization, artificially forcing the common speech and the elevated language into the same linguistic mold, and incidentally playing havoc with recognized orthographic principles. It is noteworthy that *'t* (Kethib) = *'attā* (Qere) has been preserved in the text of the Old Testament, Ezek. 23:43 and Psa. 74:6.

49. *kym* (# 2:3, etc.), "today, now," **kay-yām*. Cf. Nos. 27 and 31, Ch. II, No. 4.[40] Also note the South Arabic series: *ym, ymt, ymtn,* parallel to *ywm, ywmt,* and *ywmtn.*

50. *my* (# 2:3, etc.), "who ?," *mî.*

51. *'bdk* (# 2:3/4, etc.), "thy servant," **'abdak,* Biblical *'abd^{e}kā.* The consonantal text of the Bible preserves the shorter popular form of the suffix current in the late pre-exilic period. The Massoretic pointing implies the longer more literary form (and is based on older manuscripts in which the final vowel was indicated in the orthography by *he*[41]). The process of levelling through has operated in two directions in the Biblical text. The problem will be discussed at length in the Excursus.

52. *ky* (# 2:4, etc.), "that," *kī.*

53. ⌈'⌉*bdh* (# 2:5), "his servant," *'abdô.* Note the use of *he* as a *mater lectionis* to indicate final *ô,* as in the Meša' Stone and the Siloam Inscription.

54. *yd'th* (# 2:6, # 3:8), "thou hast [not] known it." The suffix (*ô*) is retrospective.

55. *hwš'yhw* (# 3:1), "Hoshaiah," **hawši'yahū.*

56. *dwh* (# 3:7), "sick," **dawē.*

57. *šlḥk* (# 3:7), "thy sending," **šolḥak* or the like. On the suffix see No. 51.

58. *ḥyhwh* (# 3:9), "as Yahweh lives," **ḥayyahwē.* The contraction in the orthography is instructive. Cp. the full form *ḥy yhwh* (# 6:12), **ḥay yahwē.*

whether etymologically long or short, accented or unaccented, will be indicated in the orthography, *if it is pronounced.* Cp. for example, *llh* (Ch. III, No. 41), where the final *ā* is unaccented (and originally short), but nevertheless indicated by *he.*

[40] For the form **yām,* cf. Ginsberg, *BJPES* III (1935), p. 79; Albright, "Ostracon C 1101 of Samaria," p. 215, n. 1.

[41] Contrary to Kahle, *The Cairo Geniza,* London, 1947, pp. 95 ff., and references there.

59. *nsh* (# 3 : 9), " [no one] has essayed (?)," **nissā*. The context is very difficult. The root *nsy* in Biblical Hebrew has the meaning, "try, test, tempt," but hardly, " try, attempt."

60. *'yš* (# 3 : 9/10), "man," *'īš*. If the reading and the interpretation are correct, then the *yodh* is a true internal *mater lectionis*, representing *ī*. However, the context is obscure, cf. No. 59, and for idiomatic usage, *'dm* would be preferred (as in # 4 : 5/6). The word regularly appears as *'š* in the Siloam Inscription (No. 25), but does not occur elsewhere in the Lachish Letters. Under the circumstances, it cannot be determined whether or not this word actually is *'īš*, " man."

61. *ly* (# 3 : 10), " to me," *lî*.

62. *'ly* (# 3 : 11, # 4 : 4), " to me," *'ēlay*.

63. *qr'ty* (# 3 : 12), " I have read," **qara'tî*.

64. *'th* (# 3 : 12), " it," *'ōtô*.

65. *m'wmh* (# 3 : 13), "anything" (?), Biblical *mᵉ'ūmā*. Dr. Albright suggests that the original form of this word may have been **mahŭmahŭ*, an indefinite pronoun developed from the interrogative pronoun (cf. Ugar. *mh*) by reduplication, quite as in the case of such a form as Acc. *manman*. We could then draw the equation: **mahŭmahŭ* > **măhūmăh* > **mă'ūmăh* (by dissimilation) > *mᵉ'ūmā*. The Lachish form would most nearly reflect the **mă'ūmăh* of this series. The spelling here is to be explained just as in the case of *y'wš* (cf. No. 46). That is to say, the aleph tended to quiesce in popular pronunciation leaving a virtual diphthong. The spelling with both *aleph* and *waw* would then be partly historical, partly phonetic. The reading is not certain, however.

66. *mṣrymh* (# 3 : 16), " to Egypt," **miṣraymā*.

67. *hwdwyhw* (# 3 : 17), " Hodaviah," Biblical *hôdawyāhū*, LXX, Ωδουια, Οδουια. The meaning and vocalization are uncertain.

68. *'nšw* (# 3 : 18), " his men," **'anašêw* or **'anašaw*. The suffix certainly was pronounced *-*êw* in Israelite (cf. No. 1), but it may have been *-*aw* in Judahite, since the diphthong of the construct plural was preserved in the Southern dialect (*-*ayhū* > *-*aw*). Nevertheless the singular form of the suffix has been levelled through in both dialects, so that *-*ahū* > -*aw* > -*ô* occurs in Judahite as well as Israelite (along with -*ehu* and -*ew*, cf. No. 26). The plural form *-*êw* may have been extended to the Southern dialect. This is implied in the writing -*yw* in the Massoretic text. The *yodh* must be a *mater lectionis*, and here represents *ê*.[42] In other words, the " kethib " of the Massoretic text

[42] The *yodh* cannot be explained as an instance of historical spelling (**ayhū* > **ayū* > *aw*), because if it were, then it would appear in pre-exilic texts (when

represents the Israelite (and possibly general) pronunciation, **-êw*. The Massoretic pointing, on the other hand, suggests the old Judahite (?) vocalization **-aw*. The problem is discussed further in the Excursus. In this case either reading is possible.

69. *šlḥh* (# 3:21, # 16:3?), "he has sent it," **šalaḥô*.

70. *'śh* (# 4:3), "[thy servant] did," **'aśā*.

71. *ktbty* (# 4:3), "I wrote," **katabtî*.

72. *byt hrpd* (# 4:5), "Beth-ha-Rapid" (?). The first element is to be read *bayt*. Although the form is construct, the diphthong remains uncontracted. In the Lachish Letters, all diphthongs are preserved, whether or not they occur under accent.

73. *'yn* (# 4:5), "there is not," **'ayn*.

74. *lqḥh* (# 4:6), "he took him," **laqaḥô*.

75. *wy'lhw* (# 4:6/7), "and he brought him up," **waya'lehū*. Note that the vowel of the suffix (*ū*) is indicated in the orthography: i.e., when the final vowel was pronounced, it was written.

76. *h'yrh* (# 4:7), "to the city," **ha'īrā*. The *yodh* may be an internal *mater lectionis*, cf. No. 60. Nevertheless a variant form is possible, **'ayr* or the like. Compare the plural forms *'ārīm* and *'ᵃyārīm* (?), Jud. 10:4.

77. *šmh* (# 4:8), "thither," **šammā*.

78. *nḥnw* (# 4:11), "we," *naḥnū*.

79. *nr'h* (# 4:12), "we do [not] see," *nir'ē*.[43]

80. *'zqh* (# 4:12/13), "Azeqah," Biblical *'ᵃzēqā*.

81. [*šl*]*ḥt* (# 5:4, # 9:3?), "thou hast sent." If the restored text is correct, the reading should be **šalaḥt* or the like. The 2nd m. s. perfect afformative occurs in two different forms in the consonantal text of the Bible: ת- and תה-. (Cp. the suffix forms ך- and כה-). The final vowel had already been lost in the popular speech (as in Aramaic, though note the form in the Aramaic of the Bible), but was preserved as an older and more elegant form in the literary language. The Massoretes normalized the longer form throughout the text of the Old Testament, producing the anomalous pointing תָ-. See also the discussion of this matter in the Excursus.

presumably it was still pronounced, or had only recently been lost). Needless to say it does not appear until after the introduction and general spread of internal *matres lectionis*. To regard it simply as an orthographic sign of the plural formation, is an *ad hoc* explanation without parallel and without justification.

[43] On the interpretation of this word in context, cf. Ginsberg, "Lachish Ostraca New and Old," p. 11, and in rebuttal, Albright, "The Lachish Letters after Five Years," p. 21.

82. *mh* (# 5:9), "what," *mā*, or possibly **măh* (cf. Ugar. *mh*).

83. *y*⸢*y*⸣*ṭb* (# 5:9/10), "he will benefit, do good to," **yayṭib*, following Albright's reconstruction.[44]

84. *yr'* (# 6:1), "may [Yahweh] cause [my lord] to see," **yar'*, or the like.

85. *hzh* (# 6:2), "this." Cf. Nos. 21 and 40.

86. *spry* (# 6:4), "the letters of," **sipray*. See the discussion in Ch. II, No. 32, and III, No. 29. There is no evidence for the contraction of diphthongs in Judahite until a later period.

87. *hnh* (# 6:5), "behold!", Biblical *hinnē*.

88. *dbry* (# 6:5), "the words of," **dabray*.

89. *ydyk*[ ] or *ydyk*⸢*m*⸣, "your hands," **yadayk* or **yadaykim*. The diphthong would be preserved in either case, before the suffix.

90. *ydy* (# 6:7), "the hands of," **yaday*.

91. '[*lyhm*] or '[*lhm*] (# 6:9), "to them." The former reading is preferable, the latter possible. The letters are not sufficiently clear to determine what the actual spelling is.

92. *t'św* (# 6:9), "you do," **ta'śū* or the like.

93. *'lhyk* (# 6:12/13), "thy God," **'elōhayk*.

94. *n'śh* (# 9:8), "we shall do (?)," **na'śē*.

95. *ml'kh* (# 13:1), "work," Biblical *m*^e^*lā'kā*.

96. *btš'yt* (# 20:1), "in the ninth," Biblical *t*^e^*šī'īt*. The *yodh* may be an internal *mater lectionis* here, or we may have a bi-form ending in *-*iyyat*.

97. *ywṣ'* (# 21:3/4), "he will bring forth," **yawṣi'*. The reading is not at all certain.

The epigraphic evidence for Hebrew orthography indicates that before the 9th century, Hebrew was written in a purely consonantal script. In agreement with Phoenician principles of spelling, final vowels were not indicated in the orthography. Inscriptional data from the early period is limited, but examples of this defective writing are to be found in the Gezer Calendar from the 10th century, cf. Nos. 2 and 3.

Some time after the 10th century (but in all probability by the middle of the 9th), a system of final *matres lectionis* was introduced, and from that time on, all final vowels were indicated in the orthography (in both Northern and Southern dialects). The scheme adopted was the same as that used in Aramaic and Moabite (cf. Chs. II and III).

[44] "The Oldest Hebrew Letters: The Lachish Ostraca," p. 15, and "A Reëxamination of the Lachish Letters," pp. 16-17.

The final vowel $\bar{\imath}$ was represented by *yodh*: Nos. 15, 19, 28, 45, 50, 52, 61, 63 and 71.

The final vowel $\bar{u}$ was represented by *waw*: Nos. 5, 32, 33, 39, 55, 67, 75, 78 and 92.

The final vowel $\bar{a}$ was represented by *he*: Nos. 11?, 16?, 17, 18, 22, 30?, 36, 38, 44?, 59, 65?, 66, 70, 76, 77, 80, 82 and 95.

The final vowel $\bar{e}$ was represented by *he*: Nos. 12?, 21, 40, 47, 56, 58, 79, 85, 87 and 94.

The final vowel $\bar{o}$ was represented by *he*: Nos. 20?, 23?, 43, 53, 54, 64, 69 and 74.

Final vowels are always indicated in the orthography, medial vowels almost never. The few exceptions, where medial *matres lectionis* seem to appear, all date from the 6th century. Since internal *matres lectionis* already had appeared sporadically in Aramaic inscriptions more than 100 years earlier, the possibility of their use in Hebrew must be recognized. None of the following examples, however, is absolutely certain: Nos. 42, 60, 76 and 96. It is to noted that in every case, the medial vowel is $\bar{\imath}$, designated by *yodh*.

While there is relatively little epigraphic material from North Israel, dialectal differences are easily discernible. The most important of these for orthographic analysis is the contraction of diphthongs. Note the following cases of contraction: *ay* > ê, Nos. 1, 4, and 13; *aw* > ô, No. 7.

In the Southern dialect, however, diphthongs remained uncontracted in all positions.

The diphthong *ay* was represented by its consonantal element, *yodh*: Nos. 6, 34, 37, 41, 58, 62, 66, 72, 73, 83, 86, 88, 89, 90, 91? and 93.

The diphthong *aw* was represented by *waw*: Nos. 24, 35, 43, 46, 55, 65, 67, 68, 97?.

Since the system of *matres lectionis* was not used in Hebrew before the 9th century, and since that system is substantially the same as the one used in Aramaic from the beginning of that century (if not earlier), and in Moabite from the middle of the 9th century (at the latest), it can hardly be doubted that this system was borrowed by the Israelites from the Aramaeans during the course of the 9th century B. C. Because of the sharp break in Hebrew orthographic practice between the 10th and succeeding centuries, there is no possibility that the Hebrew system of vowel letters was indigenous, arising gradually out of an accumulation of historical spellings. Rather the divergence in Hebrew orthography from the traditional phonetic consonantism of Old Canaanite (as illustrated in the Phoenician inscriptions) came about through the adoption of a system of *matres lectionis* already in existence.

CONCLUSION TO THE STUDIES

THE EVIDENCE for an original principle of phonetic consonantism in Northwest Semitic orthographic practice is decisive. This principle was inherent in the Proto-Canaanite alphabet; and the South Semitic and Ugaritic systems of writing developed under the influence of the same principle. A system of purely consonantal writing was rigorously maintained in Phoenician (its alphabet being a lineal descendant of the Proto-Canaanite) until very late times, with a minimum of historical spelling. In Hebrew, the principle of phonetic consonantism was followed down to the 10th century B. C., first through the use of the Proto-Canaanite alphabet, then under the direct influence of Phoenician spelling. This circumstance, a logical inference from the history of the Israelites and their cultural and commercial relations in the 10th century, is confirmed by the orthography of the Gezer Calendar.[1]

The phonemic character of the old script had both advantages and disadvantages. It was a very simple method of writing, easily learned, and readily adapted to the needs of almost any language. It lent itself to phonetic writing, and reflected with great sensitivity dialectal variations and phonetic changes. Regular revisions in the orthography eliminated the confusion created by historical spellings. On the other hand, as Northwest Semitic continued to break down, purely consonantal writing became a more and more ambiguous form of shorthand, and in the long run was completely abandoned.

The first important modification in the Phoenician orthographic system was made, apparently by the Aramaeans, shortly after they borrowed the alphabet (ca. 11th-10th centuries B. C.). Besides adapting the alphabet to the representation of non-Phoenician phonemes (by their closest equivalents in the Phoenician alphabet), they radically altered the basic principles of spelling. A system was developed for the indication of final vowels by the signs for consonants, which were homogeneous with the vowel sounds: *yodh* for final *ī*, *waw* for final *ū*, and *he* for the remaining vowel sounds. The precise manner in which the system of *matres lectionis* originated cannot be discovered. It is clear, however, that there was not sufficient time between the borrowing of the Phoenician alphabet, and the development of *matres lectionis*, for the system

[1] The case does not turn entirely upon the Gezer Calendar, which only fixes (if our interpretation is correct) a *terminus post quem* for the shift to the use of final *matres lectionis*. The departure from Phoenician practice and the adoption of the Aramaic system of final vowel representation can hardly have occurred before or during the period of dominant Phoenician influence (10th century).

to grow spontaneously out of historical spelling. Moreover, as has been pointed out, the tendency in Phoenician writing, as also in Aramaic, was to eliminate historical spellings, not preserve them. Rather, we must suppose conscious invention and elaboration in the use of vowel letters. Isolated examples of historical spelling may have suggested the use of vowel letters (e. g., **iyă̄* > **iy* > *ī*, with preservation of the *yodh*); the consistent representation of all final vowels is the result of standardization. The same system for the representation of final vowels was used in Moabite (with minor variations) and Hebrew from the 9th century on. It is to be concluded that the center of radiation was Aram.

Evidence for the extension of the Aramaic system of vowel representation to indicate medial vowels comes from the Zinčirli inscriptions of the 8th century. It is instructive that the earliest examples do not arise from the historical spelling of contracted diphthongs, but rather from the extension of final *matres lectionis* (*yodh* and *waw*) to the medial position with the same values. This process may have begun in Hebrew in the 6th century, but very few cases occur, just as in the Aramaic of the 8th-7th centuries. Their occurrence is sporadic until the period of general diphthongal contraction in Aramaic and Hebrew. In this stage, historical spelling plays a considerable role. The use of internal *matres lectionis* already having been established, it was then natural to preserve the signs for diphthongs even after the diphthongs had contracted. In this way, the vowel letters, *yodh* and *waw*, acquired new values, *yodh* for *ê* < *ay*, *waw* for *ô* < *aw*. This usage was extended, and *waw* ultimately displaced *he* as a *mater lectionis* for *ô*. In a similar way, *aleph* (after its general quiescence at the end of syllables) developed as a *mater lectionis* for *ā* (especially in Aramaic), displacing the older *he*. Intermediate stages in this process are recognizable in Egyptian and Biblical Aramaic.

In the past, scholars dealing with orthographic problems in inscriptional material, have been overly influenced by the mixed orthography of the Massoretic Bible. This has given rise to a loose and unscientific attitude toward orthographic principles and practice. Deriving their views from the text of the Old Testament, itself a mixture of orthographic forms from every stage in the history of Hebrew spelling, scholars have approached epigraphic materials with too little respect for the spelling as found, often violating established rules of orthographic practice and producing fantastic results. Inscriptions cannot be treated in the same manner as transmitted texts with a long history of scribal revision, the orthography of which inevitably is mixed, and the vocalization of which has been normalized at a time long after the original composition. As the foregoing study has shown, orthographic patterns followed rigid laws, and like phonetic principles can be classified historically.

Intensive linguistic studies in recent years have clarified the historical development of the Northwest Semitic dialects. During the same period, epigraphic analysis has been refined to the point that most Northwest Semitic inscriptions can be dated with remarkable accuracy. These advances in our knowledge have made possible the historical study of Northwest Semitic orthography. Although many serious problems remain, and refinement of the discipline at many points is necessary, the basic principles and general outline of orthographic development are fairly clear. This discipline will contribute, negatively at least, to the future analysis of inscriptional data in Northwest Semitic. The application of orthographic knowledge may be expected to shed light on the historical grammar of the Northwest Semitic dialects, and to play an increasingly important part in the linguistic analysis of the Old Testament.[2]

[2] Professor W. F. Albright has done pioneer work in the field of orthographic analysis, as the many references to his books and articles indicate. He also has led the way in the application of the principles of historical orthography to the biblical text, isolating, in "The Oracles of Balaam," one of the ancient poems of Israel (written, as might be expected, in the consonantal orthography of the Gezer Calendar and contemporary Phoenician inscriptions); cf. Cross and Freedman, "The Blessing of Moses," *JBL* LXVII (1948), pp. 191-210, a treatment of an ancient poem along similar lines. See also Albright's "The Psalm of Habakkuk," *Studies in Old Testament Prophecy Presented to Professor Theodore H. Robinson*, Edinburgh, 1950, pp. 1-18, in which the orthographic principles of a later period (Judah ca. 600 B. C.) are applied to the text of Hab. 3.

The views of Dr. Harry Orlinsky also merit recognition. In his "The Import of the Kethib-Ḳere and the Masoretic Note on Lᵉḵâḥ, Judges 19: 13," *JQR* N. S. 31 (1940-1941), pp. 59 f., note the following: "From all the information that we have about Northwest Semitic orthography, the *scriptio plena* was at first utterly unknown; writing was consonantal. Gradually vowel letters began to come into use, at first in final position only, later also medially." Applications of orthographic principles are to be found in the following articles by Orlinsky: "On the Cohortative and Jussive after an Imperative or Interjection in Biblical Hebrew," *JQR* N. S. 31 (1940-41), pp. 371-382; "On the Commonly Proposed *lēḵ wᵉnaʿᵃḇór* of I Kings 18: 5," *JBL* 59 (1940), pp. 515-517; "The Biblical Prepositions *Táḥaṯ*, *Bēn*, *Báʿaḏ*, and Pronouns *'Anû* (or *'Ānū*), *Zō'ṯâḥ*," *HUCA* XVII (1942-43), pp. 267-292.

APPENDIX

THE ARCHAIZING INSCRIPTIONS FROM ZINČIRLI

The publication of the two Panammu Inscriptions by von Luschan and Sachau[1] immediately precipitated heated scholarly debate, which has continued to the present time, as to the precise nature of the language of the inscriptions. Great strides, however, have been made in the analysis of the texts. Sachau correctly surmised that the language belonged to the Aramaic branch of North Semitic,[2] but otherwise failed to recognize its distinctive features. D. H. Müller[3] was the first to point out that the proto-Semitic phonemes, *ḏ*, *ẓ*, *ḍ*, *ṯ*, which had fallen together with *zayin*, *ṣade*, and *shin* in Phoenician, were still preserved in the Aramaic of the Panammu Inscriptions.[4] He noted other striking peculiarities: the emphatic state (in *-a'*) did not appear in the texts, nor did the normal Aramaic absolute plurals in *-īn* and *-ān*. The plural endings of the masculine noun, on the contrary, were *-ū* and *-ī*, and he compared these with Old Babylonian forms, and more particularly with late Aramaic dialects, which dropped the final *nun*. Müller concluded that the language of the Panammu Inscriptions was an early dialect of Aramaic.

The standard handbooks of Lidzbarski[5] and Cooke[6] added little to previous contributions. In his *Ephemeris*,[7] however, Lidzbarski maintained that the language of the Panammu Inscriptions was a local Aramaic dialect, while the Bir-RKB Inscription was written in the Aramaic of the Assyrian bureaucracy, the *lingua franca* of the day.[8]

In 1907, C. Sarauw published an important study of the Panammu

[1] *Ausgrabungen in Sendschirli*, I, pp. 49-84, Plates VII-VIII. The facsimile of the Panammu I Inscription was prepared by Euting.

[2] J. Halévy, however, assigned the language to the Canaanite group; cf. "Les deux inscriptions hétéennes de Zindjîrlî," *Revue Sémitique* I (1893), pp. 138-167, 218-258, especially pp. 243 ff.

[3] "Die altsemitischen Inschriften von Sendschirli," pp. 33-70, 113-140.

[4] Nöldeke originally supported this view, "Bemerkungen zu den aramäischen Inschriften von Sendschirli," *ZDMG* 47 (1893), pp. 96-105, but later altered his position, *Die semitischen Sprachen*, 2nd ed., Leipzig, 1899, p. 33.

[5] *Handbuch der nordsemitischen Epigraphik*, pp. 440-443; for bibliography see pp. 79 ff.

[6] *A Text-Book of North-Semitic Inscriptions*, pp. 159-180.

[7] *Ephemeris für semitische Epigraphik*, I (1900-1902), pp. 57-58.

[8] The discovery of inscriptions from the 9th century in the same language shows that this was standard Aramaic all over Syria before the period of Assyrian domination.

texts.[9] He followed closely the work of Müller and Nöldeke, but insisted that the plural endings in *ū* and *ī* pointed to Assyro-Babylonian influence, and could not be connected with late Aramaic forms.

S. Ronzevalle reviewed the literature on the subject in an article published in 1909.[10] He dealt with the problem of the language on the basis of the orthography of the inscriptions. He held that the language of the Panammu texts was fundamentally the same as that of the Bir-RKB Inscription, and that the apparent differences were due to differences in orthographic practice. The Panammu Inscriptions were written defectively, in the Phoenician tradition, while Bir-RKB was written in standard Aramaic orthography. His principal contribution was to focus attention on the problem of Aramaic orthography. His conclusions are, for the most part, untenable.[11]

J. Friedrich, writing in 1922,[12] dealt with the morphological peculiarities of the texts. He adopted Müller's views with regard to the masculine plurals in *-ū* and *-ī*, but pointed out that there was no evidence for the preservation of final short vowels in these inscriptions. It may be pointed out in passing that his late date for the loss of final short vowels in other Northwest Semitic dialects is untenable.

Among the most important recent studies of the Panammu Inscriptions is Poebel's, *Das appositionell bestimmte Pronomen der 1. Pers. sing.* (1932).[13] His work, while overly ingenious at times, adds many new insights into difficult passages. His conclusions have particular merit, because they are consistent with the established principles of Aramaic orthography, a factor too often disregarded by the earlier students of the problem.

The latest treatments are those of F. Rosenthal[14] and H. L. Ginsberg.[15] Rosenthal follows in part the views of Ronzevalle, holding that the language of the Panammu texts is standard Old Aramaic, and that differences are due to orthography. Ginsberg elaborates the views of Lidz-

[9] "Zu den Inschriften von Sendschirli," *ZA* 20 (1907), pp. 59-67.

[10] "La langue des inscriptions dites de Hadad et de Panammū," *Florilegium ou recueil de travaux d'érudition dédiés à Monsieur le Marquis Melchior de Vogüé*, Paris, 1909, pp. 519-528.

[11] Final vowel letters regularly are indicated in the orthography, cf. Ch. II. See also Ginsberg, "Aramaic Studies Today," p. 236.

[12] "Der Schwund kurzer Endvokale im Nordwestsemitischen," pp. 3-14.

[13] No. 3 in the *Oriental Institute of the University of Chicago Assyriological Studies*, Chicago, 1932, pp. 43-49.

[14] *Die aramaistische Forschung*, pp. 1-71 *passim*, esp. p. 57. Valuable bibliographical notes are included in his discussion of the early Aramaic inscriptions.

[15] "Aramaic Dialect Problems," *AJSL* 50 (1933), pp. 1-9; *AJSL* 52 (1935-36), pp. 95-103; "Aramaic Studies Today," *JAOS* 62 (1942), pp. 229-238.

barski, maintaining that the Panammu Inscriptions are written in the local Zinčirli dialect, the language of the Ba'ririm,[16] while the Bir-RKB is in the official Assyrian-sponsored Aramaic of the 8th century. His refutation of Rosenthal's position is convincing, but on the other hand, his own conclusions are not entirely acceptable. While making many sound contributions to the elucidation of the texts, his orthographic analysis requires revision.[17] Furthermore, it is now clear that standard Old Aramaic was the common language of the Aramaeans in Syria, and that Assyrian officialdom simply adopted for administrative use a dialect already dominant in the Aramaic speaking world.

The linguistic situation in Šam'al (= *y'dy*) may be sketched roughly as follows. By the 12th century, Aramaean tribes were making serious incursions into the civilized areas of North Syria. Under Tiglath-Pileser I (1114-1076 B. C.), the Assyrians were able to hold them in check, but by the 10th century, Aramaean princes were in control everywhere in North Syria. Their city-states extended from the Euphrates to the Mediterranean, except for a narrow corridor along the sea coast where the Phoenicians remained in power. For the next two centuries the Aramaeans held firmly to their possessions. Throughout that area, and during the whole period, Aramaic was the official language of the royal inscriptions, of commercial transactions, and undoubtedly the spoken language of most of the people.

Conditions at Šam'al fit into the general picture, with certain exceptions, and local variations. There were apparently two strata in the population of *y'dy*: one, the older group of native inhabitants (i. e., the *mškbm*) who may have continued to speak a Canaanite dialect; the other, the dominant group of newer settlers, who spoke Aramaic (i. e., the *b'rrm*).[18] Furthermore, a royal inscription from the 9th century (the Kilamuwa Inscription),[19] is written in standard North Canaanite. It also preserves accurately the purely consonantal orthography of the Phoenician inscriptions, contrary to the standard Aramaic spelling of the period, in which all final vowels were indicated by *matres lectionis.*

The two Panammu Inscriptions (from about 770 and 730 B. C.) represent a new departure. The language of these texts definitely is

[16] Cf. Ginsberg, " Aramaic Dialect Problems," pp. 3 ff. The word occurs in the Kilamuwa Inscription, lines 14-15.

[17] See Ch. II, note 54.

[18] Cf. A. Alt, " Eine syrische Bevölkerungsklasse in ramessidischen Aegypten," pp. 16-20.

[19] It is clear that Canaanite (Phoenician) influence persisted in this area for a long time, since in addition to the Kilamuwa Inscription (cf. Chapter I), we now have the Azitawadd Inscriptions from Karatepe (8th century).

Aramaic, with occasional Canaanite borrowings; but it is an Aramaic dialect the evidence for which is limited to these two inscriptions. The building inscription of Bir-RKB, who was also responsible for the Panammu II Inscription, is written in the standard Aramaic of Syria in this period, corresponding in all significant details with the Bir-Hadad Stele, the Zakir Stele, and the Sujin Stele.[20] It is therefore most likely that this was the common language of the Aramaic speaking population in Zinčirli, in the 8th century.

The evidence of the inscriptions seems to support the conclusion that the language of Panammu I and II is archaizing Aramaic,[21] a language no longer spoken, but used traditionally in the royal inscriptions of the ruling house of Šam'al. The orthography, however, conforms to contemporary Aramaic standards (with a few important deviations).

[20] For details, see Ch. II.

[21] Contrary to Ginsberg, who holds that the language of the Panammu Inscriptions was the local spoken dialect of Šam'al, "Aramaic Dialect Problems," pp. 3 ff. and 8-9. The extremely archaic features of the language make it very unlikely that it still was spoken as late as the 8th century. At the same time, there are features which suggest that later developments in the language have crept into the inscriptions. The fact that the absolute plural endings are in *-ū* and *-ī*, while the construct plural and the forms before suffixes are in *-ay*, suggests that forms of different historical levels have been mixed.

EXCURSUS

ORTHOGRAPHIC PROBLEMS IN THE MASSORETIC TEXT

A number of special problems arise in connection with tht Massoretic (Tiberian) pointing of the biblical text. The following paragraphs deal with a body of mixed forms, in which one vocalization is implied by the text (i. e., consonants and vowel letters), another by the Massoretic pointing (vowel signs).[1]

An important group of forms is the verbal afformatives and pronominal suffixes, which normally are vocalized with final *ā* (*qameṣ*): the perfect 2nd m. s. form of the verb,[2] the 2nd m. s. suffix, and the 3rd f. s. suffix with plural nouns and attached to the imperfect of the verb.

E. Sievers attacked the problem in his brilliant *Metrische Studien.*[3] Advancing metrical and orthographic arguments, he rejected the Massoretic vocalization of the 2nd m. s. suffix (*-kā*), and read instead **-ak* after singular nouns,[4] **-êk* after plural nouns, and so on.[5] On the other hand, he affirmed that in the instances where the suffix was written *-kh* (or the 2nd f. s. suffix *-ky*), the final vowel was to be pronounced.[6]

P. Kahle has amassed an enormous amount of evidence to show that the standard pronunciation of this suffix was **-k*, **-ak*, etc., and that the final vowel was pronounced only when indicated in the orthography.[7] In support of his contention he cites pertinent forms from the second column of the Hexapla of Origen,[8] the Latin transliterations of Jerome,[9]

[1] These are to be regarded as *Kethib-Qere* readings, not in the technical sense, but in the sense that two different readings are combined in the same form, the Kethib indicated in the unvocalized text, the Qere by the vowel points.

[2] The imperfect 2nd and 3rd f. pl. of the verb also occurs in two forms: one written with final *he*, the other without.

[3] E. Sievers, *Metrische Studien I. Studien zur hebräischen Metrik*, Leipzig, 1901, pp. 324 ff., also pp. 316-317.

[4] As in the prepositional forms: l^{e}*kā*, but in pause, *lāk*.

[5] Sievers made use of the Greek and Latin transcriptions then available to him. Since his time the evidence has been multiplied many times.

[6] He regarded these as historically correct forms, examples of deliberate archaizing preserved in the text for metrical reasons.

[7] P. Kahle, *The Cairo Geniza*, London, 1947, conveniently summarizes the material, and his conclusions, pp. 95 ff. A bibliography on the problem of the transcriptions is given in the notes.

[8] The evidence of the second column has been collected by a number of scholars, and discussed by others. Among important works on the subject are the following: E. A. Speiser, "The Pronunciation of Hebrew According to the Transliterations in the Hexapla, Chapters I-II," *JQR* XVI (1925-1926), pp. 343-382; "The Pro-

various biblical and liturgical manuscripts with the Palestinian punctuation,[10] as well as from Samaritan sources.[11] There is general agreement upon a vocalization without final *ā*; this follows the orthography (ך-) against the Tiberian pointing (ךָ-). The few exceptions in vocalization in the other sources (i. e., with *ā*) strongly imply a fuller spelling in the underlying Hebrew ms. (*-kh*) rather than the possibility of alternate vocalizations of the final *kaph*.

Kahle concludes that the Tiberian and Babylonian pointing of the suffix (ךָ and ך respectively) is an artificial "hyper-correction" made under the influence of the Arabic grammarians.[12] This view, however, is quite unnecessary. We are dealing with an inner Hebrew development. The longer form of the suffix was native to old Hebrew, and survived in elevated speech and literary works. The shorter form developed in the popular speech at a very early date (with the dropping of the final *ā̆*, which is to be regarded as *anceps*). The present Massoretic text represents a mixture of these forms, both of which have been extended throughout the Bible. The short form is preserved in the orthography, the long form in the vocalization.[13] The orthography was standardized, clearly on the basis of manuscripts in which the short form predominated.[14]

nunciation of Hebrew Based Chiefly on the Transliterations in the Hexapla (Chapter II- cont'd)," *JQR* XXIII (1932-1933), pp. 233-265; "The Pronunciation of Hebrew Based Chiefly on the Transliterations in the Hexapla (Chapter III)," *JQR* XXIV (1933-1934), pp. 9-46. M. Margolis, "Transliterations in the Greek Old Testament," *JQR* XVI (1925-1926), pp. 117-125; he reviews the work of F. Wutz, *Die Transkriptionen von der Septuaginta bis zu Hieronymus*, Leipzig, 1925. A. Sperber, "Hebrew Based upon Greek and Latin Transliterations," *HUCA* XII-XIII (1937-1938), pp. 103-274. E. Brønno, *Studien über hebräische Morphologie und Vokalismus*, Leipzig, 1943.

[9] These are collected in Sperber's "Hebrew Based upon Greek and Latin Transliterations."

[10] See the references in Kahle, *The Cairo Geniza*, pp. 96 ff. For the material from the sources, cf. Kahle, *Masoreten des Westens* II, Stuttgart, 1930, pp. 66-95; I, Stuttgart, 1927, p. 6 of the Hebrew text.

[11] Cf. Kahle, *The Cairo Geniza*, p. 97 for references.

[12] This is Kahle's view, *The Cairo Geniza*, p. 100, and compare discussion on pp. 78-86.

[13] Occasional exceptions simply indicate that the generalizing process was not carried out with complete consistency. This is especially true of the unvocalized text which still preserves many of these doublets. Cf. Sperber, "Hebrew Based upon Biblical Passages in Parallel Transmission," *HUCA* XIV (1939), pp. 153-249, *passim*.

[14] This is the case with the Nash Papyrus, which though preserving a more fully written text than the Massoretic Bible, has a short form of the 2nd person m. s. suffix. For the standard treatment of the Nash Papyrus, see S. A. Cook, "A Pre-Massoretic Biblical Papyrus," *Proceedings of the Society of Biblical*

The vocalization, however, was based on manuscripts in which the long form was common.[15] In the newly discovered Dead Sea Scrolls, there is now decisive evidence for both traditions. It is noteworthy that the short forms predominate in the fragments from the Pentateuch (and the Habakkuk Scroll), while the Isaiah Scroll (DSIa) follows the tradition, in which the longer forms had more or less levelled through.[16]

What has been said about the 2nd person s. suffix applies equally well to the perfect 2nd person m. s. of the verb (i. e., *qāṭaltā* type), and the 3rd f. s. suffix (*-hā*). The evidence again indicates a dual tradition, in which the short form predominates in the orthography, while the long form is standard in the vocalization. The imperfect forms of the verb, 2nd and 3rd f. pl., are even more instructive. Here the orthography preserves the longer form for the most part (*תִּקְטֹלְנָה), but the considerable number of exceptions (especially in the Pentateuch) shows that the short form existed and was used. In the vocalization, the long form is extended throughout the text.

In addition to forms in final *ā* (dropped in the popular language, preserved in the literary tongue), there are forms with final *ī* which fall into the same category. The 2nd person f. s. suffix appears in the orthography as *-k* and occasionally as *-ky*. In this case the short form consistently is represented in the vocalization. This also is true of the 2nd person f. s. perfect of the verb (*-t* along with *-ty*). There is no reason to doubt that both forms derive from an original Hebrew ending in *ī*.

The failure on the part of the Massoretes to recognize the existence of these doublets in Hebrew resulted in the present confusion in the biblical text. The numerous instances where the vocalization does not correspond to the orthography can only be explained on the basis of a dual tradition, not on the basis of defective orthography (i. e., reading

Archaeology, XXV (1903), pp. 34-56. On the date, see now W. F. Albright, "On the Date of the Scrolls from 'Ain Feshkha and the Nash Papyrus," *BASOR* # 115 (1949), pp. 10-19, and the literature cited there.

[15] This is implied by the evidence from the Greek transliterations. In a number of cases the Greek gives the reading -χα where the Massoretic text has ך (normally this is represented in the Greek by -χ); the implication is that the Hebrew *Vorlage* was written כה-. The evidence is to be found in Sperber, "Hebrew Based upon Greek and Latin Transliterations," pp. 197 ff.; and Brønno, *op. cit.*, pp. 195-200, 202. These transliterations come from a time when the text was more or less standardized; nevertheless some variation in the representation of the suffix is noticeable, and the Greek renditions apparently are based upon a text in which the longer form of the suffix occurred more frequently.

[16] See *The Dead Sea Scrolls of St. Mark's Monastery*, I, ed. by M. Burrows, New Haven, 1950, *passim*.

a final vowel not indicated in the spelling).[17] This stricture applies as well to final "short" or "unaccented" vowels. The system of *matres lectionis* to indicate final vowels was introduced into Hebrew at a time when final short vowels (case endings, etc.) had already been lost. Those final vowels which were preserved (whether originally long or short) after the loss of case endings regularly were indicated by vowel letters. There are no demonstrable exceptions to this in the historical data.

A related problem is that of the 3rd m. s. suffix with plural nouns: Massoretic ָיו-. A mixture in forms is involved, the orthography implying a reading, **-êw* or the like, while the vocalization is *-āw*. Albright has maintained that the historically correct vocalization of this form is **-êw*, and that the reading *-āw* is the result of Aramaic influence.[18] This contention undoubtedly is correct for the pronunciation of North Israel, where the contraction of diphthongs was very early and preceded the syncope of intervocalic *he*: **-ayhū* > *êhū* > *êw*.[19] This formation may well have been extended to Judahite, just as the 3rd m. s. suffix with singular nouns (*-ô*) seems to have been. The spelling יו in the Massoretic text seems to support this contention.[20]

On the other hand, the normal development of the suffix in Judahite would have resulted in the form *-āw* < (**-ayū*) < **ayhū*.[21] It is at least

[17] An important reservation must be made with regard to examples of defective archaic orthography preserved in the biblical text. Before the 9th century B.C., no final *matres lectionis* were used, and all forms, distinguishable only by the final vowel sound, fell together. In that period, the doublets discussed in this section were spelled in the same way, and in an authentic poem of the 10th century might be pronounced either with or without the final vowel. The appearance of the short form of a doublet of this kind cannot be regarded as a criterion for archaic orthography. Nor can isolated instances of defective writing be taken as evidence for an early date of composition; these are better taken as scribal errors. What is required is a concentration of examples in a poem, which in addition bears other marks of archaic origin; cf. Albright, "The Oracles of Balaam," "The Psalm of Habakkuk," Cross and Freedman, "The Blessing of Moses."

[18] Albright, "The Gezer Calendar," p. 22.

[19] On the date of this contraction, see Harris, *Development of the Canaanite Dialects*, pp. 29 ff.- The evidence from Ugaritic, Amarna and Egyptian transliterations is conclusive for the contraction of these diphthongs in Canaanite during the Bronze Age.

[20] The *yodh* cannot be regarded as a case of historical spelling for **-ayhū* > **ayū* > *-āw*, since it is not written in the forms with third person suffix after plural nouns in the inscriptional material. Cf. Ch. IV, No. 68.

[21] As already shown, there is no evidence for the contraction of diphthongs in Judahite before the Exile. The form in the Lachish Letters (Ch. IV, No. 68) may be read either *-āw* or **êw*. The archaic form יהו- (Hab. 3: 10, Job. 24: 23) is also ambiguous, since it may be read either **-ayhū* (following Judahite pronunciation) or *-êhū* (following Israelite, later Judean and Massoretic pro-

possible that the Massoretic vocalization derives from the Judahite pronunciation, while the orthography represents the North Israelite reading. We must suppose however a general extension of the *-*êw* form in the orthography, and a similar, subsequent levelling through of the -*āw* form in the vocalization.[22]

A brief outline of the later development of Hebrew orthography may be appended to this study. Three phases may be distinguished. In the first period, from the Exile to the time of Herod the Great, there was a general increase in the use of internal *matres lectionis.* With the contraction of diphthongs, *yodh* and *waw* received new values, *ê* and *ô* respectively; *waw* gradually replaced *he* as the sign for *ô* in the final position. During the same period, *aleph* quiesced generally and was pressed into service as a *mater lectionis* for *ā*.[23] The fullest development of *plene* writing was achieved during the Maccabaean Era (ca. 100 B. C.).[24]

During the Rabbinic period, strenuous efforts were made to fix the orthography of the biblical text (i. e., the consonants and vowel letters). A thoroughgoing revision of the spelling was undertaken, presumably on the basis of much older manuscripts (and/or manuscripts which conserved the old defective tradition). The result was a considerable modification of the excessively *plene* writing of the Maccabaean period, harking back to the orthographic styles of the 5th–3rd centuries B. C. The later parts of the Old Testament seem to have been revised syste-

nunciation). Note also doubtful forms without *yodh,* listed in *GK,* § 91, 1. The pronunciation -*āw* was general by the time of the Hexaplaric transcriptions. In addition, the occurrence of the form -*ôhī* (Psa. 116: 12, and not infrequently in DSIa, as also in three cases in the Hexapla, -αυι, Brønno, *op. cit.,* pp. 200 f.) suggest that the Aramaic ending was attached secondarily to the form -*āw.*

[22] The Massoretes did not alter the text which they received (i. e., the consonants and vowel letters), but they attempted to standardize the vocalization of the text. They minimized real differences in orthography by fixing the pronunciation of certain forms and then extending it throughout the text. A limited parallel to this may be found in the Massoretic pointing of the suffix forms with plural nouns in Biblical Aramaic.

[23] The use of *aleph* as a *mater lectionis* developed extensively in Aramaic, after the quiescence of aleph in the final position (in the emphatic state of nouns in particular). Its use in the Massoretic text is quite limited: note the form of the fem. suffix in Ezek. 41: 15, ֶיהָא–, and in DSIa, *passim.*

[24] Wellhausen suggested this almost eighty years ago, *Der Text der Bücher Samuelis,* pp. 17 ff. The point was demonstrated by Albright on the basis of the Nash Papyrus (cf. "A Biblical Fragment from the Maccabaean Age: the Nash Papyrus," pp. 145-176), which he now dates in the latter part of this period, i. e. in the first century B. C. The Dead Sea Scrolls, the early date of which may be considered as certain, provide definitive corroboration of these views.

matically on the basis of the conservative spelling practices of the Pentateuch manuscript tradition, as is evidenced by the fact that the latest books (Daniel, for example) were put into orthography which is actually older than the date of the writing of the books itself! In any case, the consonantal text of the Old Testament was fixed substantially as we have it today, in the Rabbinic period.

During the final period, the different schools of the Massoretes were active, developing systems for the vocalization of the text of the Old Testament. The Tiberian School was successful in displacing the others (during the 9th century A. D.) and its system of pointing became official. The Massoretes did not attempt to alter the text which they received. However, they did standardize the vocalization of the text, following for the most part the implications of the orthography. Occasionally, in the interests of uniformity, they disregarded the plain evidence of the unpointed text.

BIBLIOGRAPHY OF WORKS CITED

Albright, W. F., "Further Observations on the Name *Yahweh* and its Modifications in Proper Names," *JBL* XLIV (1925), pp. 158-162.

———, "Notes on Early Hebrew and Aramaic Epigraphy," *JPOS* VI (1926), pp. 75-102.

———, "A Neglected Hebrew Inscription of the Thirteenth Century B. C.," *AfO* V (1929), pp. 150-152.

———, *The Archaeology of Palestine and the Bible*, 3rd ed., New York, 1935.

———, "The Inscription from Gezer at the School in Jerusalem," *BASOR* #58 (1935), pp. 28-29.

———, "A Supplement to Jeremiah: The Lachish Ostraca," *BASOR* #61 (1936), pp. 10-16.

———, "The Early Evolution of the Hebrew Alphabet," *BASOR* #63 (1936), pp. 8-12.

———, "Ostracon C 1101 of Samaria," *PEFQS* 1936, pp. 211-215.

———, "A Biblical Fragment from the Maccabaean Age: the Nash Papyrus," *JBL* LVI (1937), pp. 145-176.

———, "The Oldest Hebrew Letters: The Lachish Ostraca," *BASOR* #70 (1938), pp. 11-17.

———, "A Reëxamination of the Lachish Letters," *BASOR* #73 (1939), pp. 16-21.

———, "The Lachish Letters after Five Years," *BASOR* #82 (1941), pp. 18-24.

———, "New Light on the Early History of Phoenician Colonization," *BASOR* #83 (1941), pp. 14-22.

———, *Archaeology and the Religion of Israel*, Baltimore, 1942.

———, "A Votive Stele Erected by Ben-Hadad I of Damascus to the God Melcarth," *BASOR* #87 (1942), pp. 23-29.

———, "Two Little Understood Amarna Letters from the Middle Jordan Valley," *BASOR* #89 (1943), pp. 7-17.

———, "The Copper Spatula of Byblus and Proverbs 18: 18," *BASOR* #90 (1943), pp. 35-37.

———, "The Gezer Calendar," *BASOR* #92 (1943), pp. 16-26.

———, "The Oracles of Balaam," *JBL* LXIII (1944), pp. 207-233.

———, "Postscript to Professor May's Article," *BASOR* #97 (1945), p. 26.

———, "The Chronology of the Divided Monarchy of Israel," *BASOR* #100 (1945), pp. 16-22.

———, "The Phoenician Inscriptions of the Tenth Century B. C. from Byblus," *JAOS* 67 (1947), pp. 153-160.

———, "The Early Alphabetic Inscriptions from Sinai and their Decipherment," *BASOR* #110 (1948), pp. 6-22.

———, "On the Date of the Scrolls from 'Ain Feshkha and the Nash Papyrus," *BASOR* #115 (1949), pp. 10-19.

———, "The So-called Enigmatic Inscription from Byblus," *BASOR* #116 (1949), pp. 12-14.

———, "Some Important Recent Discoveries: Alphabetic Origins and the Idrimi Statue," *BASOR* #118 (1950), pp. 11-20.

———, "The Psalm of Habakkuk," *Studies in Old Testament Prophecy Presented to Professor Theodore H. Robinson*, ed. by H. H. Rowley, Edinburgh, 1950, pp. 1-18.

Alt, A., "Eine syrische Bevölkerungsklasse in ramessidischen Aegypten," *Zeitschrift für Ägyptische Sprache und Altertumskunde* 75 (1939), pp. 16-20.

Bardowicz, L., *Studien zur Geschichte der Orthographie des Althebräischen*, Frankfurt a. M., 1894.

———, "Das allmähliche Ueberhandnehmen der *matres lectionis* im Bibeltexte," *Monatsschrift für Geschichte und Wissenschaft des Judenthums* 38 (1894), pp. 117-121, 157-167.

Barth, J., *Sprachwissenschaftliche Untersuchungen zum Semitischen*, Leipzig, 1907.

———, *Die Pronominalbildung in den semitischen Sprachen*, Leipzig, 1913.

Bauer, H., "Die כלמו Inschrift aus Sendschirli," *ZDMG* 67 (1913), pp. 684-691; *ZDMG* 68 (1914), pp. 227-228.

———, "Ein aramäischer Staatsvertrag aus dem 8. Jahrhundert v. Chr. Die Inschrift der Stele von Sudschin," *AfO* VIII (1932), pp. 1-16.

Bauer, H., and Leander, P., *Historische Grammatik der hebräischen Sprache des Alten Testamentes*, Halle a. S., 1922.

———, and ———, *Grammatik des Biblisch-Aramäischen*, Halle a. S., 1927.

Bea, A., "Die Entstehung des Alphabets," *Miscellanea Giovanni Mercati* VI, 1946, pp. 1-35.

Bergsträsser, G., *Hebräische Grammatik* (*Wilhelm Gesenius' hebräische Grammatik* 29th ed.), I: *Einleitung, Schrift- und Lautlehre*, Leipzig, 1918.

Birnbaum, S., "The Dates of the Gezer Tablet and of the Samaria Ostraca," *PEQ* 1942, pp. 104-108.

———, "On the Possibility of Dating Hebrew Inscriptions," *PEQ* 1944, pp. 213-217.

Blake, F. R., "The Word זדה in the Siloam Inscription," *JAOS* 22 (1901), pp. 55-60.

———, "The Development of Symbols for the Vowels in the Alphabets Derived from the Phoenician," *JAOS* 60 (1940), pp. 391-413.

Böhl, T., "Die Sichem-Plakette," *ZDPV* 61 (1938), pp. 1-25.

Bowman, R. A., "The Old Aramaic Alphabet at Tell Halaf," *AJSL* 58 (1941), pp. 359-367.

———, "Aramaeans, Aramaic, and the Bible," *JNES* VII (1948), pp. 65-90.

Brockelmann, C., *Syrische Grammatik*, Berlin, 1899.

———, *Grundriss der vergleichenden Grammatik der semitischen Sprachen, I: Laut- und Formenlehre*, Berlin, 1908.

———, "Zu den Inschriften des Königs Kalumu," *Sitzungsberichte der Preussischen Akademie der Wissenschaften* (Berlin), 1911, pp. 1142-1146.

———, "Kanaanäische Miscellen," *Festschrift Otto Eissfeldt*, Halle, 1947, pp. 61-67.

Brønno, E., *Studien über hebräische Morphologie und Vokalismus*, Leipzig, 1943.

Burrows, E., "The Tell Duweir Ewer Inscription," *PEFQS* 1934, pp. 179-180.

Burrows, M., ed., *The Dead Sea Scrolls of St. Mark's Monastery*, I: *The Isaiah Manuscript and the Habakkuk Commentary*, New Haven, 1950.

Cantineau, J., "Remarques sur la stèle araméenne de Sefiré-Soudjin," *Revue d'Assyriologie* 28 (1931), pp. 167-178.

Chomsky, W., "The History of our Vowel-System in Hebrew," *JQR* N. S. 32 (1941-42), pp. 27-49.

Chwolson, D., "Die Quiescentes הוי in der althebraeischen Orthographie," *Travaux de la troisième session du Congrès International des Orientalistes, St. Pétersbourg 1876*, II, St. Petersburg and Leiden, 1879, pp. 457-490.

Clermont–Ganneau, Ch., *Recueil d'Archéologie Orientale*, VI, Paris, 1905.

Cook, S. A., "A Pre-Massoretic Biblical Papyrus," *Proceedings of the Society of Biblical Archaeology* XXV (1903), pp. 34-56.

Cooke, G. A., *A Text-Book of North-Semitic Inscriptions*, Oxford, 1903.

Cowley, A., *Aramaic Papyri of the Fifth Century B. C.*, Oxford, 1923.

Cross, F. M. Jr., and Freedman, D. N., "The Blessing of Moses," *JBL* LXVII (1948), pp. 191-210.

———, and ———, "The Pronominal Suffixes of the Third Person Singular in Phoenician," *JNES* X (1951), pp. 228-230.

Diringer, D., *Le iscrizioni antico-ebraiche palestinesi*, Florence, 1934.

———, "The Palestinian Inscriptions and the Origin of the Alphabet," *JAOS* 63 (1943), pp. 24-30.

———, "The Dating of Early Hebrew Inscriptions (The Gezer Tablet and the Samaria Ostraca)," *PEQ* 1943, pp. 50-54.

———, "Note on the Dating of Early Hebrew Inscriptions," *PEQ* 1945, pp. 53-54.

Driver, G. R., "Notes on the Aramaic Inscription from Soudschin," *AfO* VIII (1933), pp. 203-206.

———, "Brief Notes," *PEQ* 1945, pp. 5-9.

Driver, S. R., *Notes on the Hebrew Text and the Topography of the Books of Samuel*, 2nd ed., Oxford, 1913.

Dunand, M., "Nouvelle inscription phénicienne archaïque," *RB* 39 (1930), pp. 321-331.

———, "Inscription phénicienne de Byblos," *Kêmi* IV (1931/1933), pp. 151-156.

———, "Une nouvelle inscription énigmatique," *Mélanges Maspero* I, Fasc. 2 (1935-38), pp. 567-571.

———, *Fouilles de Byblos*, I (*Atlas*), Paris, 1937; II (*Texte*), Paris, 1939.

———, "Spatule de bronze avec épigraphe phénicienne du XIIIe siècle," *Bulletin du Musée de Beyrouth* II (1938), pp. 99-107.

———, "Stèle araméenne dédiée à Melqart," *Bulletin du Musée de Beyrouth* III (n. d.), pp. 65-76.

———, *Byblia Grammata*, Beyrouth, 1945.

———, "A propos de la stèle de Melqart du musée d'Alep," *Bulletin du Musée de Beyrouth* VI (1946), pp. 41-45.

Dussaud, R., *Les monuments palestiniens et judaïques*, Paris, 1912.

———, "Les inscriptions phéniciennes du tombeau d'Aḥiram, roi de Byblos," *Syria* V (1924), pp. 135-157.

———, "Dédicace d'une statue d'Osorkon I par Eliba'al, roi de Byblos," *Syria* VI (1925), pp. 101-117.

———, Review of P.-E. Guigues, "Pointe de flèche en bronze a inscription phénicienne," and S. Ronzevalle, "Note sur le texte phénicien de la flèche publiée par M. P.-E. Guigues," in *Syria* VIII (1927), pp. 185-186.

Ewald, H., *Ausführliches Lehrbuch der hebräischen Sprache*, 8th ed., Göttingen, 1870.

Février, J. G., "Remarques sur le Calendrier de Gezer," *Semitica* I (1948), pp. 33-41.

Fischer, A., "Zur Siloahinschrift," *ZDMG* LVI (1902), pp. 800-809.

Flight, J. W., "The Present State of Studies in the History of Writing in the Near East," *The Haverford Symposium on Archaeology and the Bible*, ed. by E. Grant, New Haven, 1938, pp. 111-135.

Friedrich, J., "Der Schwund kurzer Endvokale im Nordwestsemitischen," *Zeitschrift für Semitistik* I (1922), pp. 3-14.

———, *Kleinasiatische Sprachdenkmäler*, Berlin, 1932.

———, "Eine phönizische Inschrift späterer Zeit aus Byblos," *OLZ* 38 (1935), pp. 348-350.

———, "Kein König פלמה in der Stele von Sudschin," *ZA*, NF 9 (1936), pp. 327-328.

———, "Zur Einleitungsformel der ältesten phönizischen Inschriften aus Byblos," *Mélanges Dussaud*, Paris, 1939, pp. 39-47.

———, "Eine altphönizische Inschrift aus Kilikien," *Forschungen und Fortschritte* 24 (1948), pp. 76-79.

Friedrich, J., and Landsberger, B., "Zu der altaramäischen Stele von Sudschin," *ZA* NF 7 (1933), pp. 313-318.

Friedrich, J., Myer, G. R., Ungnad, A., and Weidner, E. F., *Die Inschriften vom Tell Halaf*, Berlin, 1940.

Gaster, T. H., "The Tell Duweir Ewer Inscription," *PEFQS* 1934, pp. 176-178.

———, "The Archaic Inscriptions," *Lachish II, The Fosse Temple*, Oxford, 1940, pp. 49-57.

Geers, F. W., "The Treatment of Emphatics in Akkadian," *JNES* IV (1945), pp. 65-67.

Gesenius, W., *Geschichte der hebräischen Sprache und Schrift*, Leipzig, 1815.

———, *Scripturae Linguaeque Phoeniciae*, Leipzig, 1837.

Ginsberg, H. L., "Aramaic Dialect Problems," *AJSL* 50 (1933), pp. 1-9.

———, "על תעודות לכיש" (English Title: "Observations on the Lachish Documents"), *BJPES* III (1935), pp. 77-86.

———, "Aramaic Dialect Problems II," *AJSL* 52 (1935-36), pp. 95-103.

———, "Lachish Notes," *BASOR* # 71 (1938), pp. 24-27.

———, "A Further Note on the Aramaic Contract Published by Bauer and Meissner," *JAOS* 59 (1939), p. 105.

———, "Lachish Ostraca New and Old," *BASOR* # 80 (1940), pp. 10-13.

———, "Aramaic Studies Today," *JAOS* 62 (1942), pp. 229-238.

———, "MMŠT and MṢH," *BASOR* # 109 (1948), pp. 20-22.

Ginsburg, C. D., *Introduction to the Massoretico-Critical Edition of the Hebrew Bible*, London, 1897.

Gordon, C. H., "Lachish Letter IV," *BASOR* # 67 (1937), pp. 30-32.

———, "The Aramaic Incantation in Cuneiform," *AfO* XII (1939), pp. 105-117.

———, *Ugaritic Handbook. Analecta Orientalia* 25, Rome, 1947.

———, "Azitawadd's Phoenician Inscription," *JNES* VIII (1949), pp. 108-115.

Grant, E., "Découvert épigraphique à Beth Šemeš," *RB* 39 (1930), pp. 401-402.

Gressmann, H., *Altorientalische Texte und Bilder zum Alten Testamente*, Tübingen, 1909; 2nd ed., Berlin and Leipzig, 1926.

Grimme, H., *Grundzüge der hebraeischen Akzent- und Vokallehre*, Freiburg, 1896.

Guigues, P.-E., "Pointe de flèche en bronze a inscription phénicienne," *Mélanges de l'Université Saint-Joseph* XI (1926), pp. 323-328.

Guy, P. L. O., and Engberg, R. M., *Megiddo Tombs*, Chicago, 1938.

Halévy, J., "Les deux inscriptions hétéennes de Zindjîrlî," *Revue Sémitique* I (1893), pp. 138-167, 218-258.

———, "Les inscriptions du roi Kalumu," *Revue Sémitique* XX (1912), pp. 19-30.

Harris, Z., *A Grammar of the Phoenician Language,* New Haven, 1936.

———, *Development of the Canaanite Dialects,* New Haven, 1939.

Hehn, J., "Die Inschrift des Königs Kalumu," *Biblische Zeitschrift,* 1912, pp. 113-124.

Honeyman, A. M., "Epigraphic Discoveries at Karatepe," *PEQ* 81 (1949), pp. 21-39.

Horsfield, G., and Vincent, L. H., "Une stèle Égypto-Moabite au *Balou'a*," *RB* 41 (1932), pp. 417-444.

Ingholt, H., *Rapport préliminaire sur sept campagnes de fouilles à Hama en Syrie (1932-1938),* Copenhagen, 1940.

Kahle, P., *Masoreten des Ostens,* Leipzig, 1913.

———, *Masoreten des Westens,* I, Stuttgart, 1927; II, Stuttgart, 1930.

———, *The Cairo Geniza,* London, 1947.

Kallner, R. B., "שתי כתובות על גבי חרסים" (English Title: "Two Inscribed Sherds from Tell eṣ-Ṣarem"), *Kedem* II (1945), pp. 11 ff.

Kautzsch, E., *Wilhelm Gesenius' hebräische Grammatik,* 28th ed., Leipzig, 1909.

Lagarde, P., *Anmerkungen zur griechischen Übersetzung der Proverbien,* Leipzig, 1863.

Lagrange, M. J., "La nouvelle inscription de Sendjirly," *RB* NS 9 (1912), pp. 253-259.

Levi Della Vida, G., and Albright, W. F., "Some Notes on the Stele of Ben-Hadad," *BASOR* #90 (1943), pp. 30-34.

Lidzbarski, M., *Handbuch der nordsemitischen Epigraphik,* Weimar, 1898.

———, *Ephemeris für semitische Epigraphik,* I: 1900-1902, Giessen, 1902; III: 1909-1915, Giessen, 1915.

Littmann, E., "Die Inschriften des Königs Kalumu," *Sitzungsberichte der Preussischen Akademie der Wissenschaften,* 1911, pp. 976-985.

Luckenbill, D. D., "Azariah of Judah," *AJSL* XLI (1924-25), pp. 217-232.

Luschan, F. von, *Ausgrabungen in Sendschirli,* IV, Berlin, 1911.

Maisler, B., "Zur Urgeschichte des phoenizisch-hebraeischen Alphabets," *JPOS* XVIII (1938), pp. 278-291.

———, "Excavations at Tell Qasile," *BJPES* XV: 1-2 (1949), pp. 8-18, Pl. V, 1.

Marcus, R., and Gelb, I. J., "The Phoenician Stele Inscription from Cilicia," *JNES* VIII (1949), pp. 116-120.

Margolis, M., "Transliterations in the Greek Old Testament," *JQR* XVI (1925-26), pp. 117-125.

May, H. G., "Lachish Letter IV: 7-10," *BASOR* #97 (1945), pp. 22-25.

Montet, P., *Byblos et l'Égypte, Texte,* Paris, 1928; *Atlas,* Paris, 1929.

Montgomery, J. A., "Two Notes on the Kalamu Inscription," *JBL* XLVII (1928), pp. 196-197.

———, *A Critical and Exegetical Commentary on the Books of Kings, The International Critical Commentary,* New York, 1951.

Müller, D. H., "Die altsemitischen Inschriften von Sendschirli," *Wiener Zeitschrift für die Kunde des Morgenlandes* VII (1893), pp. 33-70, 113-140.

Nöldeke, T., *Die Inschrift des Königs Mesa von Moab,* Kiel, 1870.

———, "Bemerkungen zu den aramäischen Inschriften von Sendschirli," *ZDMG* 47 (1893), pp. 96-105.

———, *Die semitischen Sprachen*, 2nd ed., Leipzig, 1899.

Noth, M., "La'asch und Hazrak," *ZDPV* 52 (1929), pp. 124-141.

Obermann, J., "The Archaic Inscriptions from Lachish," *JAOS* 58 (1938), Supplement, pp. 1-48.

———, *New Discoveries at Karatepe*, New Haven, 1949.

O'Callaghan, R. T., "The Phoenician Inscription on the King's Statue at Karatepe," *CBQ* XI (1949), pp. 233-248.

Olshausen, J., *Lehrbuch der hebräischen Sprache*, Braunschweig, 1861.

Orlinsky, H. M., "On the Commonly Proposed *lēḵ wena'aḇôr* of I Kings 18: 5," *JBL* LIX (1940), pp. 515-517.

———, "The Import of the Kethib-Ḳere and the Masoretic Note on *lekāh*, Judges 19: 13," *JQR*, NS 31 (1940-41), pp. 59-66.

———, "On the Cohortative and Jussive after an Imperative or Interjection in Biblical Hebrew," *JQR*, NS 31 (1940-41), pp. 371-382; 32 (1941-42), pp. 191-205, 273-277.

———, "The Biblical Prepositions *Táḥaṯ, Bēn, Bá'aḏ*, and Pronouns *'Anû* (or *'Ānū*), *Zōṯāh*," *HUCA* XVII (1942-1943), pp. 267-292.

Peiser, F. E., "Aus dem Kaiserlich ottomanischen Museum in Constantinopel," *OLZ* I (1898), cols. 5-8.

———, "Die neue Inschrift aus Sendschirli," *OLZ* XIV (1911), cols. 540-545.

Petrie, F., *Ancient Gaza*, London, 1931-34.

Poebel, A., *Das appositionell bestimmte Pronomen der 1. Pers. sing. in den westsemitischen Inschriften und im Alten Testament. Oriental Institute of the University of Chicago Assyriological Studies*, No. 3, Chicago, 1932.

Pognon, H., *Inscriptions sémitiques de la Syrie, de la Mésopotamie et de la région de Mossoul*, Paris, 1907-08.

Rahlfs, A., "Zur Setzung der Lesemütter im Alten Testament," *Nachrichten von der Königlichen Gesellschaft der Wissenschaften zu Göttingen*, Philologisch-historische Klasse, 1916, pp. 315-347.

Reisner, G. A., Fisher, C. S., and Lyon, D. G., *Harvard Excavations at Samaria 1908-1910*, Cambridge, 1924.

Ronzevalle, S., "La langue des inscriptions dites de Hadad et de Panammū," *Florilegium ou recueil de travaux d'érudition dédiés à Monsieur le Marquis Melchior de Vogüé*, Paris, 1909, pp. 519-528.

———, "Note sur le texte phénicien de la flèche publiée par M. P.-E. Guigues," *Mélanges de l'Université Saint-Joseph* XI (1926), pp. 329-358.

———, "Fragments d'inscriptions araméennes des environs d'Alep," *Mélanges de l'Université Saint-Joseph* XV (1930-1931), pp. 237-260.

Rosenthal, F., *Die aramaistische Forschung*, Leiden, 1939.

Sachau, E., "Die Inschrift des Königs Panammû von Šam/al," *Ausgrabungen in Sendschirli*, I: *Einleitung und Inschriften*, Berlin, 1893, pp. 55-84.

Sarauw, C., "Zu den Inschriften von Sendschirli," *ZA* 20 (1907), pp. 59-67.

Sievers, E., *Metrische Studien* I. *Studien zur hebräischen Metrik*, Leipzig, 1901.

Smend, R., and Socin, A., *Die Inschrift des Königs Mesa von Moab*, Freiburg, 1886.

Speiser, E. A., "The Pronunciation of Hebrew According to the Transliterations in the Hexapla, Chapters I-II," *JQR* XVI (1925-26), pp. 343-382.

———, "The Pronunciation of Hebrew Based Chiefly on the Transliterations in the Hexapla (Chapter II—cont'd)," *JQR* XXIII (1932-33), pp. 233-265; (Chapter III), *JQR* XXIV (1933-34), pp. 9-46.

Sperber, A., "Hebrew Based upon Greek and Latin Transliterations," *HUCA* XII-XIII (1937-38), pp. 103-274.

———, "Hebrew Based upon Biblical Passages in Parallel Transmission," *HUCA* XIV (1939), pp. 153-249.

Stade, B., *Lehrbuch der hebräischen Grammatik*, Leipzig, 1879.

Starkey, J. L., "Excavations at Tell el Duweir, 1935-6," *PEFQS* 1936, pp. 178-189.

———, "Excavations at Tell ed-Duweir," *PEFQS* 1937, pp. 228-241.

Sukenik, E. L., "הערה לחרס מתל אץ–צארם" (English Title: "Note on the Sherd from Tell eṣ-Ṣarem"), *Kedem* II (1945), p. 15.

Sukenik, Y., על חרס העופל, *BJPES* XIII (1947), pp. 115-118.

Taylor, W. R., "The New Gezer Inscription," *JPOS* X (1930), pp. 79-81.

———, "Some New Palestinian Inscriptions," *BASOR* #41 (1931), pp. 27-28.

Thureau-Dangin, F., Barrois, G., Dossin, G., and Dunand, M., *Arslan-Tash*, Paris, 1931.

Torczyner (Tur-Sinai), H. (*et al.*), *Lachish I. The Lachish Letters.* London, 1938.

———, "כתובות השלוח לוח גזר וחרס העופל" (English Title: "The Siloam Inscription, the Gezer Calendar and the Ophel Ostracon"), *BJPES* VII (1939-40), pp. 6 ff.

———, "להבנתו של לוח גזר" (English Title: "A New Interpretation of the Gezer Calendar"), *BJPES* XIII (1946-47), pp. 1-7.

Torrey, C. C., "The Zakar and Kalamu Inscriptions," *JAOS* 35 (1915-17), pp. 353-369.

Wellhausen, J., *Der Text der Bücher Samuelis*, Göttingen, 1871.

Wutz, F., *Die Transkriptionen von der Septuaginta bis zu Hieronymus*, Leipzig, 1925.

Yeivin, S., "The Palestino-Sinaitic Inscriptions," *PEQ*, 1937, pp. 180-193.

———, *The History of the Jewish Script* (Hebrew), I, Jerusalem, 1939.

Zolli, E., "La tavoletta di Gezer," *Biblica* 27 (1946), pp. 129-131.